The Practicing Life

SALLY HOWELL JOHNSON

Kirk House Publishers
Minneapolis, Minnesota

The Practicing Life

Sally Howell Johnson

ISBN – 10: 1-933794-79-8

ISBN – 13: 978-1-933794-79-2

Kirk House Publishers, PO Box 390750, Minneapolis, MN 55439
www.kirkhouse.com
Manufactured in the United States of America

Contents

Introduction

For some time now I have been exploring the word *practice*. As someone who was born, reared, and trained in the church, I have heard of the importance of spiritual disciplines my whole life. But I have to admit that, for me, the word *discipline* ranks alongside the word *diet*. It seems to smack of denying myself pleasure, grunting and bearing up under pain, and all manner of piety that just doesn't fit who I am or how I want to live out my spiritual walking in the world. The word *practice* works much better for me. It is a word the Buddhists have used for centuries and they are some of the kinder, calmer people I know. It has also worked well for those who have chosen to live in religious community—nuns, monks, and other people who have dedicated themselves to actually trying to live in the Way of Jesus by living together, sometimes in small spaces. In community, they practice what it means to live together with all the complexities of being human. So, over the last few years when I have spoken of prayer, meditation, scripture study and other spiritual acts we are encouraged to do, I have chosen to use the word *practice*.

Frankly, I probably like the word *practice* because, by its very nature, it implies that though I may get better at what I am doing, I will never fully arrive. For me, this is an appealing idea. For instance, I have tried over and over again to read through the Bible cover to cover and have never made it. Not once. I have read most of the books many times and other sections lots of times. Having been a seminarian, I did have to read, study, and understand its writing, historical context, and meaning. But unlike many of my brothers and sisters in the faith whom I hold in high regard, I can quote very few scripture passages by book and verse. I can, however, tell some of the really great stories in the scriptures. I can even act them out and add my own social commentary if invited. While I may at some point want to create a practice of reading through the Bible from Genesis to Revelation, I have a feeling that it will always remain in the realm of Webster's definition for the verb

of *practice*: "to perform an activity or exercise repeatedly or regularly in order to improve one's proficiency."

Over the last five years, I have written a daily blog on the website for the church I am privileged to serve. It is something I started to do as an encouragement to the congregation during Advent. Every weekday during the four-week season that leads up to the celebration of Christmas, I wrote a short reflection. My hope was that people would pause from what they were doing during one of the busiest times of the year, read the words I had crafted, and then use those words to help them reflect on their own spiritual life. For this reason I called the blog, "Pause." I never intended to have it be more than twenty reflections that might ground people for what amounted to less than five minutes reading time.

But what I learned in writing those twenty reflections is that when you begin a practice, sometimes you get hooked. When I came to the end of that season and the time for these Advent reflections had melted into Christmas carols, I had begun a practice—a practice that had helped me pray, meditate, study scripture, and reflect on the presence and movement of the Holy in my life. And like any relevant and important practice, I found I had to continue it. For my own spiritual growth. For my own wholeness and healing.

So five years have passed, and more than a thousand reflections have been written. It truly has become a practice that grounds me. I have heard from people near and far who check in daily or sporadically and those connections are always a blessing. When that happens, I feel as if I am in an even larger practice that has created a community of people I know well and those I will never meet. The messages sent to me often have something to do with how my experience has given words to their own, how what I have written has helped them see and experience the presence of the Sacred in their own life. This, of course, brings me great joy while also carrying with it a huge sense of humility.

Because the majority of my life has been spent in the church, I see that one of the greatest unmet opportunities I have seen over the many years is the profound need to create an environment where people can learn to develop a reflective life. We are very good at providing intellectual content through Bible and book studies. People come to soak that up. We are also fairly adept at providing opportunities for people to develop small group friendships and social contact, some that lead to spiritual formation. We are very good at organizing and structuring systems to govern and do the business of the institution in great hope of attracting more to our places of worship and communal life.

But how and where do people know what to do with their daily experience of miracle and mediocrity? How do people see the Holy in their every-day, working, living, playing lives and be empowered to talk about it? How do we not only help people stay awake to the movement of the Sacred, but also take the time to reflect on these experiences, finding words to tell their own gospel story?

My answer to this question is that it is, I believe, a matter of practice—a practice of staying awake, of being present, of paying attention, of being in community, of telling our stories, of living our lives with the deep knowing that we are a part of a web that is so intricate it is pure mystery. We share the journey with the human ones we encounter every day and the other creatures that speak without words of the One who brought them to be. Those with two legs, with four legs, and those with wings. Those that slither and those that root themselves in the soil and those that rise on the wind to spread their seed in unplanned-for places. How we provide the space, the sacred space, for all the searching people to develop as reflective spiritual travelers is, I believe, the great work of the church. It is, in fact, the great work of what it means to be human. We are, after all, the ones with words. We are the storytellers for the on-going telling of creation's unfolding.

In the following pages, I have selected reflections on various ways of being a practicing people. There are invitations to be awake, to revel in community, to be

a traveler, to honor one's path. There are stories of encounters with God in places that are predictable and surprising. Most of all there are words that, hopefully, encourage readers to develop their own practice, their own reflections—a practice that allows them to find a place of grounding in the One who breathed them into being and delights in the twists and turns of their life.

It is an invitation to The Practicing Life.

Bud or Blossom?

And the day came when the risk to remain tight in the bud was greater than the risk to bloom. – ANAIS NIN

These evolving autumn days are urging me to reflect on the summer that is now only a memory. This reflection is enhanced by the small notebooks and pieces of paper on which I have jotted down words said or read, ideas that came to me in the humidity and heat. You see, I have this habit of writing down things that, at the moment, seem paramount but on further reflection can cause me to furrow my brow.

I do this "jotting," I think, in a concerted effort to keep myself from writing in a journal as many people do. I guess I think that if I simply write these things down on 3x5 notecards or on the back of a napkin, I won't give the thoughts too much weight or take myself too seriously. After all, what might happen if someone would find my journal and read words I found important? So, while I may have started countless, beautiful journals, they are mostly left free of any real, important thoughts in favor of the jotting, scrap method.

So on this autumn day I took the opportunity, while under the guise of cleaning out my book bag, to look over the little bits of this and that which had grabbed my attention, lifted my spirit, or just seemed like something with which I should spend more time. The quote of Anais Nin above was tucked among those scribbles, some of which have lost their meaning to me as the temperatures have turned cooler.

Risk. Frankly, I don't like to think much about risk. And yet it infuses all our lives and is the stuff of growing, of deepening our lives in any significant way. I probably like to stay in "bud" form rather than take the risk of blooming. It is safe. I know the landscape, understand the soil. Blooming requires being seen, being known for

what I really am. And sometimes I don't like the petals I can put on display in the world. Petals that are less than kind. Petals that make judgments and are gossipy. Petals that don't make room for other bloomers around me. It is easy to focus on these more negative blooms.

But I have been thinking about risk these past several days. Our older son is having a life adventure, camping and surfing up the West Coast. He is traveling with his dog and making it up as he goes along. It seems, from the mother point-of-view, to be filled with risks. And yet, it is so much a part of moving from bud to blossom, finding the next thing in his life after college. The adventure has allowed him to have rich and enlivening experiences which have included surfing while seals looked on as he was surrounded by a pod of dolphins. This is not a "bud" but a "blossom" experience.

As I think about our faith stories they are all about people who could no longer stay in the bud. Moses. Esther. Abraham. Mary. Ruth. John. Paul. Jesus. Each came to the point, over and over again, when staying in the bud would have been to deny God's call on their lives.

And so they took a risk. Many times blossoming led to beautiful and rich experiences. Other times it led to tragedy and hardship. The same holds true for us. To remain in the bud means never coming into our fullness. Each breath, each moment, each day, each year holds out bud and blossom. The question is, what will we choose?

What is longing to blossom in your life these autumn days? What risks are held in the promise of the bud? As the leaves begin to turn and fall, may the buds you are holding find the courage to take a risk.

Practice:

Carry a 3x5 card around for a week. Write down ideas, words, or thoughts that come to you. At week's end read what you have written. Do any of these jots lead you to risk? Which might lead you from bud to blossom? Follow it!

The Other

We live in a world that makes much of difference. Messages come at us, sometimes at dizzying speed, about all the ways humans are different....race, ethnicity, religion, social status, education....the list is exhaustive, and sometimes exhausting. Recently, I read a poem by 20th century Welsh poet, R.S.Thomas which describes an experience of one person awake at night on one side of the Atlantic wondering about an imagined being on the other side of the world who may also be tossing and turning in the room of insomnia. In his poem he imagines allowing prayers to "break on him" not for just the hours of sleeplessness but for all eternity. In these nighttime hours, the waves of prayer seem to float with ease across the many differences the world might offer up, even across the vastness of ocean. While I believe Thomas was probably speaking in this poem of his understanding of the movement of the Holy, his words dredge up in me that deep sense of connection I often have, at fleeting moments, to those I have never met, those whose differences may be visible or invisible, those who live "across the sea" of my experience.

This feeling often comes to me in large groups of people. Looking out across a wide expanse of humanity at, say, a sporting event or concert, I think about the fact that I do not know these people. I have no idea of the intricacies of their lives, what they love, what troubles them. I search the faces to look for familiar features that do not materialize. At the same time, I realize that the faces that look back do not know me. They do not know that my favorite color is green, that I love poetry, that I will choose pie over roast beef any day.

And yet here we all are. In this mix of people traveling the Earth together at the same time. Each of us making decisions and hoping for the best. Each of us seeking meaning and a way of being known, of being loved, of being heard. We all do it

in different ways, but the desire still wells up in us in similar ways. This somehow brings me great comfort when the specifics of my personal problems or the weight of my daily rounds threaten to overwhelm my sensibilities.

While R.S. Thomas thinks of the ultimate being that waits at the edges of the sea of prayers, I think of all those other beings, much like myself, who lie awake in the night worrying about their children or dreaming of a solution to a hovering problem. I think of the mothers, in the wee hours of the night, nursing their infants as I once did, trying to keep awake through sheer will. I also think of those mothers who cannot feed their children, who don't know where the next meal will come from, and the despair that lives in them. While the poet imagines the prayers washing up on the shore of the Sacred, I imagine the person, on the other side of the world, looking into the night sky, gazing at the full, white moon, just like I am. Are they imagining a person who lives a life unlike their own yet with the same hope for a better world for their children, their grandchildren? Are they imagining me?

This may all sound silly, but it is something that swooshes in on me every now and then. This feeling of traveling on this spinning planet with so many fragile, yet hopeful, beings seems such a gift. To feel the rush of the realization of all "the others" that are spinning with me seems rich, deep, not unlike a prayer.

Practice

Have you ever had this experience, this feeling? If not, I offer this to you: The next time sleep eludes you in the middle of the night, begin to think of all the people on the other side of the world who are already living a day you have not yet been given. Imagine them moving about their daily lives, just as you will when the sun rises. Imagine the ways their lives are so different, yet similar, to your own. Imagine sending them all the hopes you have for goodness in your life and the lives of those you love. Allow the prayers of your heart to connect with the hearts who, perhaps, do not speak the same language or share your faith tradition. Allow the rising and falling of your breath, the words of your prayers, to wash upon the shore of "the others." It is my suspicion that in doing so, those same prayers will also break upon "the Other" for this hour, this day, this year, for eternity.

Regenerating Force

Thank you Father for your free gift of fire.
Because it is through fire that you draw near to us everyday.
It is with fire that you constantly bless us.
Bless this fire today,
With your power enter into it.
Make this fire a worthy thing,
A thing that carries your blessing.
Let it become a reminder of your love.
A reminder of life without end.
– MASAI PRAYER

Today I read with interest an article about what is already happening in our beloved Boundary Waters Canoe Area as the fires that have been burning there begin to die out. Jim Williams who reports on birds in the *Minneapolis Star Tribune* spoke of the numbers of winged ones that are being seen in the charred forests. While many will not return for some time, others like the black-backed woodpecker are already hard at work eating up the insects that follow a fire. According to ornithologists, others will show up in spring: Eastern bluebirds, Wilson's warblers, kestrels, flickers, common yellow-throats. These birds will flock into this recently burned area in numbers higher than usual.

It is often difficult for us to realize that this area loved so for its pristine beauty and wildness gets its life, or rebirth of life, from fire. While humans may have built houses and other dwellings in these places that can be threatened by fire, the forest itself needs the fire to continue to be the place we know and love. It is strange to think that what we often consider destructive is what really brings new creation. While some of the wild life will move on, much will return and still others will arrive to surprise the land with their presence. It is how it all works."*Fire has been the dominant regenerating force in those forests for tens of thousands of years,*" says Gerald Neimi, an ornithologist with Natural Resources Research Institute.

Imagining the regenerating power of this fire nudged me to think of all the many times rebirth comes out of what seems like fire and chaos. While not literal fire, these experiences can threaten to overwhelm us. How often in organizations, what seems like a "fire" rushes through the ways we've always done things and sets us on our heads. While it seems the flames are lapping at our feet, it is difficult to feel anything but panic and fear. But when the experience of fire begins to ebb, we often can have the capacity to see things in new ways, welcome fresh ideas or new people in, let go of growth that no longer serves us well. I've certainly seen this happen in schools, government, churches, any organization that can dig its heels into the soil of what they believe to be tradition or stability.

Out of the trail of the fire, often known as change, we begin to see things in ways that might serve us better than we ever imagined before. Like the newly introduced birds who will call the BWCA home in a few months, we can have the opportunity to look around and see things we've never seen before. We have the chance to build new nests, maybe ones that fit who we are now more than who we once were.

Any of this make sense to you? Is there a place in your work life or spiritual life that could benefit from a cleansing fire? The Masai prayer speaks of fire as blessing. It is a challenging notion but perhaps a useful one. Where, in you, is new life longing to rise up out of what has been destroyed?

I offer this prayer for all who are in need of the new creation: May the One who comes to us sometimes as a gentle breeze and other times as a cleansing fire, be present this day and all days.

Blessed be.

Practice

Light a small candle. Spend time looking at its flame. Notice the colors, the way it moves when you move, how your breath effects its flickering. Repeat the Masai Prayer and allow its wisdom to work within you.

What We Love

Use the things of the world as nature needs them, but not with excessive attachment.
For it would be very displeasing to God if you were to set your heart on something of less
value than yourself. . . . People become like what they love.
– CATHERINE OF SIENA

Over the past week I have been on vacation. I have been traveling throughout the southeastern part of the country from Ohio to Georgia and back. It was a road trip with my mother that has been much anticipated. As I was preparing to leave for this respite, I was also acutely aware of the economic turmoil that has gripped our nation and the great divisions that have played themselves out in angry sound bites. Like most people, I was drawn into watching and listening as a lack of civility was being slung back and forth. It often felt like a very helpless place to be.

So, while I hoped it wasn't an act of burying my head in the sand, I looked forward to unplugging for a week of vacation, of turning off the constant sources of information that can become my daily food. Loading up the car to head south, I looked forward to conversation that would be filled with mostly reminiscences of family times, of what seems like simpler times. Settling in to the ten hour drive to Georgia from my small hometown in southern Ohio, I let go of the anxieties that could push and pull at my psyche and my spirit. It felt very good to set this intention.

As we made our way through West Virginia, I was once again startled by the beauty of this often undervalued state. The unfolding mountain ranges, filled to capacity with hardwood trees that created a blanket of rippling greens, took my breath away. As we continued to drive we seemed to free fall into the mountains of North Carolina, again, so stupendous with trees that, come fall, will create a patchwork of autumn hues that will rival the quilts made famous by the artisans of the area. Finally we drove into Georgia and through the Low Country as it

takes on a mysterious palette of waving grasses and waters interrupted by long, wooden walkways that cause people to look like miraculous walkers-on-water. Our destination of Savannah seemed to open its arms with a full southern welcome of heat, humidity, and the slow movements of people who have long moved through such temperatures and no longer fight the elements.

Along the drive we rarely listened to the radio and only tuned into television a few times. What I found was that I had slowly allowed what my eyes had pulled in—the beauty of trees ancient and new, the assurance of mountains and water, the sweet,welcoming dispositions of the people we encountered—to act as a balm. These gifts of creation had calmed and healed some place in me. I know no other way to explain it.

Catherine of Siena was a wise woman who also lived in troubled times. (And then again, which "times" know no trouble?) The words she writes about "excessive attachment" remind me of the wisdom we often associate with our Buddhist brothers and sisters. They encourage an ability to connect with what is truly of value, allowing our lives to reflect a depth that cannot be bounced around by the whims of a fragile, often fickle, world. At the same time, the words caution against trying to hold too tightly to anyone or anything in an effort to believe ourselves more in control than is ever possible.

Holding ourselves and our world gently, I have found, can result in living a more faithful, less anxious life. I don't know about you, but it is certainly my hope that I might become more like "what I love." Steadfast as the mountains. Nimble as the moving waters. Able to bend and reflect the beauty of changing seasons as the trees do. Responsive to and welcoming of the rhythm of the many climates we are blessed to experience. These are some of the gifts of both Creator and Creation which I hope will continue to inform and shape who I become in the face of both troubled and terrific times.

As this vacation draws to a quiet close, I pray I can continue to be bathed in the lessons of the landscape that has offered me its grace. When the lack of civility that seems to be our daily bread becomes too much to stomach, may I remember: Strong mountains. Tall trees. Bridges that connect. Water that holds wondrous life. And faces that register welcome and hospitality. A slower pace that allows time to revel in it all.

How about you? What do you love? How do you hope to become more like what you love?

Practice

Today choose one element of Creation you can see out your window or on your commute. Reflect on its lessons for your life. Allow it to bless you this day. Offer your thanks.

This Day

This day God gives me strength of high heaven,
Sun and moon shining, flame in my hearth,
Flashing of lightning, wind in its swiftness,
Depths of the ocean, firmness of earth.
– JAMES QUINN, S.J., ASCRIBED TO ST. PATRICK

I had it in my head that today was a good day to take the light rail train to work. It has turned cold again, but I didn't think it would be too bad. In fact I thought it would be refreshing. The rain of the weekend has now settled into solid form; a shiny ice covers most surfaces. The sky was bringing the gift of a new, flaky snow as I left to drive to the Fort Snelling station where I park my car. The wind was whipping the coats of my soon-to-be fellow travelers as I parked my car and scuttled toward the station. Not too bad, I thought. Jumping on the train, I settled back into my seat to read a few pages of my novel. Warm, toasty.

Getting off at Nicollet Mall, the wind really picked up and I began to feel the prickling sensation of genuine cold on my cheeks and began to question myself. Maybe this hadn't been such a good idea. I kept my head down, watching only my booted feet as I moved with other automatons down the mall. That's when I heard her. My eyes looked up to see a young woman, bundled in perfect Minnesota winter wear, scarf covering her neck and cheeks,backpack on her back, but a small drum in her hand. She wasn't playing for money or panhandling. She was simply walking along to her own drumbeat. I smiled.

A few blocks farther than the drumming woman, I was greeted with a hearty "good morning!" Looking up from my careful ice-dodging, I saw one of the uniformed Minneapolis ambassadors whose job it seems is to keep things tidy and to be cheerful. I returned his smile and made my now nearly frozen face muscles form a "good morning."

Then just past the friendly greeter I saw a beautiful sight: a row of little faces, a rainbow of children, all lined up looking out the window onto the mall. They were smiling and gently pounding on the window. At first I thought they were an extension of the ambassador program stationed to greet me, but then I saw what had their attention. A large riding snowblower was cleaning the newly fallen snow off the sidewalk. They were so excited by the sight that I found myself sharing in their joy. I, on the outside, wanted to run up and hug the driver on their behalf but thought better of it.

If I had driven my car to work, I would have missed these little morning gifts. Sitting in stalled traffic, creeping on icy roads bumper to bumper, I would have been denied the drumming woman, the friendly greeter, and the welcoming faces of toddlers. What a shame that would have been! Making my way on through Loring Park, I realized I was humming this song to myself:

> *This day God sends me, strength as my guardian,*
> *Might to uphold me, Wisdom as guide.*
> *Your eyes are watchful, your ears are listening,*
> *Your lips are speaking, friend at my side.*

The wisdom of St. Patrick found its way into my glorious morning!

Practice

Our brains are strengthened when we interrupt our daily patterns. What consistent rhythms in your day could benefit from a shake up? Change one of them today and notice the gifts of this shift.

Scraps of Paper

We are here to abet creation and to witness to it, to notice each other's beautiful face and complex nature so that creation need not play to an empty house.
– ANNIE DILLARD

I have a habit, some might call it a bad habit, of writing little cryptic notes to myself on small scraps of paper. Usually I put them in my pocket or slip them inside my datebook or journal. I refer to them for ideas for writing, a sermon, or just because I found the words beautiful, important, inspiring. You get the idea. In most circumstances when I am finished using them in some way, I pitch them in the trash.

Over the Christmas break, I was cleaning out some books I no longer have need of and this quote of Annie Dillard fell out of the book and onto the floor. Reaching down to pick it up, I read the words and a great smile spread across my face. This is a statement I have loved for a long time and I had forgotten it. "We are here to abet creation and to witness to it, to notice each other's beautiful face and complex nature so that creation need not play to an empty house." Let those words wash over you. Doesn't it give you a sense of purpose? Doesn't it fill you with some deep seeded joy? So, this is the answer to the question of why we are here!

I think I also love this phrase because it redeems the word "abet," meaning to support, encourage, approve, affirm. This is our work as humans: to encourage and support Creation. This is our work: to approve the beauty of the faces of those we meet, to affirm the complex nature of the humans and non-humans in our lives. What if we gave ourselves this mission statement and set goals each day to accomplish the work of our lives? Can you imagine the change it might make in the world? It is a wonderful idea to imagine coming to fruition.

There are people I have met who seem to have known that this "abetting" stuff was their life's work. They are the ones who look you right in the eye as if you are the only person with whom they would want to talk in any particular moment. Their gaze causes you to stand taller, feel more confident, be more authentically yourself. These are the people who notice things, little things, that are good and comment on them. They are almost always the ones who send a little note out of the blue to tell you they enjoyed something you did, something you said.

Still other "abettors" I know are the ones who you will find standing quietly under a tree looking up into the branches, head tilted slightly to identify the song of a bird. They are the ones who can be seen showing a small child a tiny insect on the sidewalk, passing on the importance of the work of ants, spiders, even mosquitoes. They are the ones who can be seen gazing out toward a sunset with a far off look in their eyes as if trying to become a part of the mystery and beauty of that ending moment of a day.

I want to become more of an "abettor," to follow the wisdom on this recovered scrap of paper. I want to do my work and do it well. I want to be the awe-struck audience member at this Universe play—the one who doesn't rudely whisper to my neighbor, who doesn't rattle the candy wrapper making unneeded noise, who doesn't cough so incessantly that I distract those around me. I want to be present at the play, to offer fullness of my presence for all its worth, and when the time is perfect, applaud my appreciation.

Practice

Make a commitment this day to pay attention to the faces you meet. Look people fully in the eyes. If they are wearing a name tag, address them by name. Or even better, be bold and ask their name. Tell them yours. Become an abettor in any way you can.

Looking Skyward

On the other side of the world people are experiencing a solar eclipse. I have been following it on television and online. I am always interested in these events that draw us in to the amazing workings of our Universe. They seem to provide a wake up call to my usual way of moving mindlessly past the miracles and wonders that surround me at any given moment. There has also always been that certain touch of danger about a solar eclipse instilled by elementary teachers and protecting mothers: "Don't look it directly! You"ll go blind." While I am sure there might be the possibility of damage to the eye, the warning has always ranked right up there with those given about BB guns. ("You'll shoot your eye out!")

But the solar eclipse took on new meaning and now sweet memory when several years ago our church was visited by a choir from Haiti. This choir is a part of a sister church we have supported in Port-au-Prince. Many from our congregation have traveled to this poor nation over the years to build, paint, work, and worship with these kind-hearted, faithful people. Each time those who went to help received more than they ever gave.

The Haitian choir was here in the summertime when Minnesotans love to complain about the heat. These dark-skinned, beautiful people were right at home in the sweltering summer weather. They were also here when we were to experience a total solar eclipse. We had been following the time at which the eclipse was to happen. Equipped with our pieces of paper with a small pinpoint hole punched in it, the staff of the church and the Haitian choir members headed out to view this phenomenon safely with our handmade protection fit for any third grade classroom. We stood around on the concrete with the heat reflecting on white and black skin. American English, Creole, and French filled the air as we oohed and ahhed at this gift from Creation. While we could not understand one another's words fully, we knew this: We were, all of us together, witness to a miracle, an experience of awe and mystery.

I do not remember the names of those who shared in this rare and beautiful experience with me. I am hoping that someone from our community has been able to stay in touch, knows how to reach out to them. I do not know if they are alive today or if they, like so many of their fellow citizens, have fallen victim to the horror of the recent earthquake. In a land that is poorer than anything I can imagine, I am always humbled by this nation's resilience. I still recall, in one of the many television clips after yet another tragedy, a group of people, homeless, without any personal belongings left to their name, standing together by the side of the road singing. Singing with full voices, gentle smiles on their faces, arms lifted in praise, and faces looking skyward.

I want to believe that among those singing were relatives, co-workers, neighbors, even those choir members themselves, waiting, as we all often are, for some kind of miracle.

> *No storm can shake my in-most calm,*
> *While to that rock I'm clinging.*
> *Since Love is lord of heaven and earth,*
> *How can I keep from singing?*
> – ROBERT LOWRY

Practice

There are so many places around the world that suffer. Choose one of these nations or groups of people. Write the name of this chosen country on a piece of paper—or better yet, your hand—and every time you see it, send a prayer of peace.

Antsy

People in Minnesota and like climes are getting antsy for spring. I saw several people carrying bouquets of tulips over the weekend. No doubt they were bringing some signs of this longed-for season into their homes to add color and promise. I also noticed that many of the conversations I had over the last several days somehow meandered their way to spring topics—gardening, Easter, baseball. Even the birds can now be heard trying to usher winter out the door, throwing out their welcome mat of music.

We have planted several things indoors that are helping us gauge the coming of spring. We have a long silver planter filled with herb seeds beginning to show their lovely, little, yellow-green heads. We have another pot filled with paper-whites reaching toward the brilliant February sunshine that flows through the window, reflecting off the still-white ground. And on our kitchen table is the creme de la creme—an amaryllis bulb as big as a softball digging its roots into the dirt. Planted sometime last week, it is now making a show of itself, green shoot pushing out of the gnarly bulb at what seems like an inch an hour. It is growing so quickly, it seems as if we could almost watch it, catch it in its upward movement toward becoming beautiful.

These are the little tricks we winter people allow ourselves so we can hold onto hope, so we can remember what growth feels like, looks like. I recommend it. By the time spring actually arrives, which will be much longer than we'd like, there will be the delicate flowers of paper-whites blooming in the family room. And if the amaryllis continues at the speed and power it has shown so far, our kitchen will be flooded with a flower the size of a dinner plate. These little signs of growth will carry us through the days when the melting snow will turn even dirtier as it reveals all kinds of hidden objects caught off guard by the falling snows of October.

Over the weekend, a wayward opossum returned to the backyard. This time I wasn't even concerned. I just smiled at his seeming eagerness for spring as well. He loped around the backyard looking not quite so confused, more awake, as he munched on some stray birdseed. The squirrels didn't even give him so much as a look. Perhaps we are all just getting used to one another, waiting for winter to be finished with us.

Spring is not here yet, but we are having glimpses, and that can make all the difference. On Sunday at church someone requested the lovely song by Natalie Sleeth, "Hymn of Promise." We began our singing clothed in the grays, browns, and blacks of our winter state of mind. Our voices joined together:

> In the bulb there is a flower, in the seed an apple tree;
> in cocoons, a hidden promise:
> butterflies will soon be free!
> In the cold and snow of winter
> there's a spring that waits to be,
> unrevealed until its season,
> something God alone can see.

When we finished singing, our cheeks were rosy with the promise of what is to come.

This spring we long for will be revealed in its own time, like all good gifts. Our work these days is to wait . . . and watch. And not get too antsy.

Practice

Plant something. Seeds of any kind. Buy a bouquet of flowers to add color to your life. Buy an extra bouquet, and give them to a friend or even a stranger.

Practice

The day of my spiritual awakening was the day I saw—and knew I saw—all things in God and God in all things.
– MECHTILD OF MAGDEBURG

Here we are two days into Lent. How is it going for you? Some people I know give up things for Lent—chocolate, wine, television, mostly things that give them pleasure. I've yet to hear of anyone giving up, say, spinach, Brussels sprouts, or exercise. Why do you think that is? There is a movement I've also heard of this year to give up driving to reduce one's carbon footprint. Not a bad idea, but one that would take, for most people, an incredible amount of re-orchestrating daily movement. I am sure these sacrifices all have meaning to the people who are embarking on them. I personally have never found this kind of practice helpful to my spiritual life, which is, I think, the purpose of giving something up for Lent.

Instead, for me Lent has always been a time of taking on something, something that will in some way lead me into a deeper relationship with the Holy. Taking on a new dimension of life has more power for me than giving up something like chocolate which, for me, would only make me crabby and obsessive, waiting so much for those Cadbury Easter eggs that I would miss Lent altogether. Different strokes. One year I prayed a *novena* every day using a book by Joan Chittister, OSB, called *Life Ablaze*. One Lent I made a promise of writing a poem everyday. (Nominal success, leading to some pretty bad poetry.) Another year I did *lectio divina*, a practice of reading scripture slowly, meditatively, looking for the phrase or word that seemed to speak directly to me. Of course, all these practices had limited success in living them out as most life changes we endeavor to make. But I do believe they served to give a certain intention and focus to this season which can shape us in new ways if we let it.

This year I have decided to read through the book of Ezekiel and try to create something visual as a daily practice. Ezekiel has always been one of my favorite books of the Bible. It contains the resurrection story of the Hebrew scriptures, the story of the dry bones scattered in the wilderness waiting for the Spirit to breathe over them bringing them to life once again. It is a good story to walk with in Lent, in winter days. In the midst of February and March, two of the coldest months of the year, who can not identify with the white bones, lifeless and without form? These months are filled with waiting for new life.

Lent can be, if we allow it, a time set aside for creating a practice to wake us up to the presence of the Holy. It can be a time to wander in the wilderness like Jesus did, further honing our identity, getting to know ourselves in new ways. In the process we may just come to know God in new ways as well. This might happen through giving up something. It also might happen by committing ourselves, like Mechtild, to seeing God in all things and all things in God. As I read the scriptures it seems pretty clear that this is what Jesus did. He walked around looking for God in all things...people, places, fish, bread, wine. And in the process enfolding all things in God.

Whatever the practice, or lack of one, may our walk these days lead us to a fuller knowledge of the One who walks with us, even when we do not know it.

Practice

Choose to walk into this day with an openness to seeing the Holy in all things. Pay attention to what you notice. At the end of the day make a list of all your "sightings." Give thanks.

Inside Out

All we have in life is life. Things—the cars, the houses, the education, the jobs, the money—come and go, turn into dust between our fingers, change and disappear . . . the secret of life . . . is that it must be developed from the inside out.
– JOAN CHITTISTER, *Illuminated Life*

I don't know about you but when I see the words, "the secret of life," I always perk up. Finally, someone's going to tell me the answer! Of course, we all know in part the answer to the question, "What is the secret of life?" But we want to find a short cut, a Cliff-notes version that is easier, takes less time, can be completed with fewer headaches and heartaches. Mostly we want to stay on the surface and glide along with few bumps and bruises.

But if we are really honest with ourselves we know that anything that really matters takes time, effort, commitment, sweat, and a few well-shed tears. And since life *really* matters, the secret to its living should be no exception. Do you agree? Instead of living our lives like little water bugs flitting across the surface of the water, we must go inside, deep inside, to develop the gifts of this living.

The season of Lent is an invitation to going inside, of taking the time to search within to find what has been hiding there. Lent asks us to stop what we have been doing and take a look in the mirror, perhaps take off the masks we've worn for too long and see ourselves in new ways. These forty days give us the permission to stop clinging to those things outside us that seem to give us definition (do they really?) and remember the soil in which we have been planted. Lent is not so much a time of self-denial as it is self-assessment. What temptations are luring me? What roads am I willing to walk down? How might I be more authentically both my human and divine self?

Quote from Illuminated Life *by Joan Chittister, published by Orbis Books, 2000. Used with permission.*

Lent is where the rubber meets the road. If we allow ourselves to be swept up in the gifts of this season, in this time of the year, we can come through these forty days a fuller picture of who we were born to be. And wouldn't that be a good thing? I think so. I believe the Holy One would agree. My mother has a saying: "No one ever said life would be easy. But it will always be worth it." She also says: "A hundred years from now, you'll never know the difference." But that is a thought for another day.

For this day, this first full day of Lent, I plan to allow myself to look inside. I pray I find some beautiful secrets there waiting to be discovered, secrets that will lead me to a fuller picture of my life.

Practice

Find a quiet spot where there will be no interruptions. Begin by getting comfortable in your chair, feet flat in the ground. Close your eyes and find your own breath. Breath in through your nose and slowly exhale through your slightly open lips. Allow your breath to slow to a comfortable rhythm. Notice where you hold your tension. Send your breath to that place. Imagine yourself in both your outer and inner forms. Breathe deeply and fully. Spend as much time as you can or care to developing this practice.

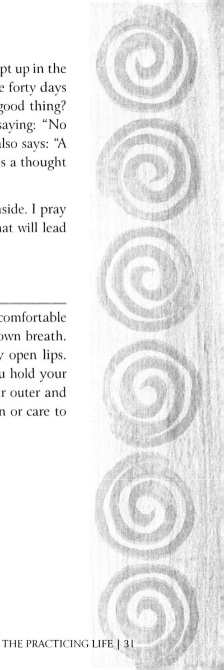

Blessed by Sunset

God said "Let there be lights in the dome of the sky, to separate day from night. Let them mark the fixed times, the days and the years and serve as luminaries in the sky, to shed light upon the earth. God made the two great lights, the greater one to govern the day, and the lesser one to govern the night. God saw how good it was. Evening came, and morning followed.
~ GENESIS 1

I am watching the sun set on the frozen lake outside my window. Dotting the water's surface are the countless ice houses that break up the sea of white stretching onto the horizon. Their mostly monochromatic colors of beige, white, and gray are punctuated every now and then with a brilliant red structure, then a bright blue one. (If I had an ice house, I'd paint it red so I could find myself in a snowstorm!) The sky is, just this minute, forming hot pink and lavender stripes that in turn reflect onto the white prairie of snow. It is an Impressionistic canvas being painted before my very eyes. Two snowmobiles are shooting across the lake—bundled up cowboys riding into the sunset.

Giant trees, oaks and maples mostly, are creating a black lace curtain against the lake. Snow clings to the branches, holding on for dear life. Up one side of the sturdy trunks the wind has glued the memory of its flight pattern. Yesterday morning I watched as a squirrel jumped from tree to tree with the ease and confidence of a trapeze artist. It made me laugh.

This noon, while eating lunch, my eyes were shocked by the sudden soaring movement of an enormous bird flying toward the center of the lake. Upon further inspection, I was blessed to recognize the brilliant white head of a bald eagle, its wings outstretched, surveying the ice below, perhaps remembering warmer times when a tasty meal lingered below. Not today, my friend. You will have to be content with your gift of flight. The eagle circled several times over the ice house villages, offering his blessing.

The sun is a half sphere of red about to dip behind the farthest side of the lake. It is creating a deep yellow and orange that brushes color onto the white clouds, the edges now tinged with gold leaf, as if the Great Artist added that last touch just for dramatic effect. The now purple clouds are moving south as the wind picks up and, no doubt, the temperature plummets. But wait, the sky has gone completely fuchsia! The sun seems to be saying, "I'm not quite finished with this day." Oh, brilliant Sun, you always have the last word!

What possible reason is there that I have been given such a gift of beauty, of mystery, of wonder? Since I cannot answer this immense question, I will say only, "Thank you. Thank you. Thank you."

Practice

Think through all the people, sights, sounds, smells, tastes, experiences for which you can exclaim, "Thank you. Thank you. Thank you." Make a list. Memorize it. Save it for a day when you most need it.

Yes

Christ, all love, you speak one word to us: Yes. Yes, I am with you. Yes, I always will be. Yes, in deepest sorrow. Yes, when you have lost your way, your sight, yourself. Yes, when you don't know what to do and when there is nothing you can do; Yes, today and tomorrow. – JULIAN OF NORWICH

Over the weekend I had the privilege of "being the voice" of Julian of Norwich, a fourteenth century mystic whose words seem to be long before their time. Our sanctuary choir presented a lovely musical setting of her words. Her writing seems miraculous to me given the climate in which she lived, given the fact that she was a woman in a church ruled by those who would have much preferred she remain silent. Her life was plagued with great pain, both physical and spiritual. And yet she had the clarity of experience of the Holy that rings throughout time. Her words reflect a broader understanding of God than the common church language, not only of her time but also ours, might allow. She used multiple images of God and blurred the often exclusively male language attributed to speaking of the Sacred.

But even more than those gender nouns and pronouns, her understanding of our relationship with the Holy One carries such acceptance, such grace, such gentleness. As I read her words during the concert, my eyes took in the faces, the beautiful faces of those gathered. I wondered about those who were listening. How were they experiencing these words? Did they seem foreign? Did a God whose one word to us is "Yes" align with the one they learned of in Sunday school, in sermons, in scripture? I also thought of all those people I knew who have been so wounded by the church and its use of words. Those who cannot find a home in any faith community. Those who think that the rhetoric they often hear on radio and television spoken with anger and vengeance, voices claiming to speak for Jesus, is all there is.

To these people and to all people I offer Julian's experience of the Holy when she writes:

Yes, on this corner of my good earth and wherever your feet may take you. Yes, to the end of the earth and the eternity of time. Yes, for you are never abandoned. You are forever the unforsaken, the beloved, a cradled child. Mine. And my word to you is singular: Yes.

I am reminded that the "Yes" of God carries us into an understanding of the Way in which Jesus of Nazareth walked in the world. At every turn he offered a "Yes" to those on the margins, those left out, those who were hungry, those who didn't know where to turn. Like Julian, he embraced the "Yes" of the Holy in his own life and then extended that affirmation to all he met.

My saints long before you clung to my "Yes" in circumstances unimaginable, amid joys inexpressible and griefs unbearable. And I was enough for them. I was their "Yes," and ever I shall be for you.

Practice

Spend some time rereading these words of Julian. How do they feel? To whom might you offer them? How can you pray them? If her words are helpful, search out more of her beautiful writing.

Twice Blessed

An early morning walk is a blessing for the whole day. – HENRY DAVID THOREAU

We have a gigantic amaryllis bulb that has been growing in a pot on our kitchen table since Valentine's Day. Over the last two weeks it has developed five saucer-sized blossoms of delicate pinks and creamy white. None bloomed at the same time. They each had their own coming-out day. We, the observers, had to keep a trained eye to the next miracle emerging from our dining table. Over the course of several days, another show of floral beauty dazzled us as we consumed cereal or soup.

Yesterday as I was inwardly lamenting the blossoms that have now withered and fallen off, I noticed what seems like another shoot of green pushing its way up the side of the nearly two-foot stalk that housed these flowers. This morning I saw that it had grown another several inches. I marveled: Could it be possible that yet another shoot would give birth to even more pink and white color? My husband registered his skepticism. It didn't seem probable that we could be blessed twice by one gnarly looking—OK, ugly—bulb. Who knows? But we will continue our breakfast and dinner vigil, watching with untrained, yet hopeful, eyes.

This waiting and watching got me thinking about the many ways in which we receive unexpected blessings. This morning on my walk I was serenaded by a choir of red-winged black birds. These birds which most often go unnoticed amid their flashier feathered friends, seemed to be singing seduction songs across tree branches. I felt blessed to be present to their love lurings—not something I expected on a Monday morning.

A few steps along the same path I passed a man walking his dog. The man was in a hurry. The dog wasn't. His mutt body, weighing in someplace between beagle and corgi, exuded the happiness of walking in a place so full of new life and good scents. As my human form met the other and his canine crossing the small foot bridge, the dog stopped right in his tracks, looking me square in the eyes. I swear I think he smiled! I know I did as his owner gave a gentle tug on his leash to get him moving. I walked on having been given what felt like a dog blessing.

For the longest time humans have tried to relegate blessings to certain places— churches for instance—but we might as well give in. Blessings are surrounding us all the time. To bless means: the infusion of something with holiness, divine will, or one's hope. In the amaryllis plant I continue to see the divine will to give birth, to be beautiful, to save my human self from the grayness of winter days. In the song of the red-winged black birds I heard the hope of summer yet to come. In the eyes of a leashed dog I saw unconditional acceptance and maybe even love.

Twice blessed? Oh, no—so many times blessed!

Practice

Spend the day as someone who blesses. Say "Bless you" out loud or under your breath. Hold out your hand gently toward what you want to offer a blessing. Bless human, creature, plant . . . everything!

Sufficient

Last week—I swear it—I saw a butterfly flying around in our backyard in the middle of March in Minnesota. It swooped near the side porch and then flitted away into the marvelous sunshine. I shook my head in wonderment. Where did it come from? How had it come to such fullness with winter days so recently in the past? My husband didn't really believe my sighting. And then, some minutes later, as we were beginning a walk on our block, a butterfly—was it the same one?—flew right across our path. We looked at one another and laughed at this curious sight so early in the year.

This butterfly seemed to be flying as fast as it could. Perhaps such movement was necessary given the chill that still existed in the air. Soon enough we will see butterflies doing the languid hastelessness that is their nature and often so foreign to ours. On the purple flowers that bloom in our garden meant to attract these lovely insects, we will have the seasonal opportunity to learn from the butterfly. If we can be quiet enough, if we can keep our minds from racing to the next thing we are "supposed" to be doing, if we can keep our limbs from twitching with constant activity, we, too, can learn hastelessness. I have a sense there is much to be gleaned from this non-activity. Feeling the full force of the sun on our bodies, we might be lured into a creative moment of dreaming something beautiful. We might learn how to slow our breathing to a place of prayer. We might even allow our eyes to see as the butterfly sees—up close and personal. If nothing else, we might simply bring our blood pressure to a lower reading, which is always a good thing.

Living into a recognition of the fullness of life in each moment is also a gift. Instead of experiencing the moment as just the step to the next, and then the next, doesn't allow us to recognize the blessing of each breath, each heartbeat which we do not initiate. They happen because we are alive. The sufficiency of each moment eludes us: this moment is enough to keep me going, to keep me living.

I am preaching to myself here, I know. I have just decided to take a few days off to recharge my batteries before heading into the busyness of Holy Week, and I am finding it difficult to just be in the moment. My mind is jumping around from thought to thought, detail to detail. I keep remembering "what I've forgotten to do." Ever have days like that?

Perhaps if I had wings, beautifully colored wings, I could flap them in a quiet, easy rhythm until my mind slowed down to a calmer pace. Then I could sit as long as I wanted gently flapping and breathing, in and out, in and out, until hastelessness set in. Finally I could stay in one place as long as need be until my spirit could catch up with my flying body.

It is a wonderful thing to imagine. I hope it is even possible without wings. I'm going to give it a try until I come into the sufficiency of this moment.

Practice

Find fifteen minutes in your day. Find a place you'd like to spend that fifteen minutes. Do not bring anything to that place—certainly not a phone or a computer. Simply be in this place for fifteen minutes. If it suits you, extend your time. Be haste-less.

Easter Came Early

I came that you might have life, and have it abundantly. – JOHN 10:10

Signs of spring are everywhere. As the snow has slowly melted into the ground, the greenness of spring is pushing its way up through rich, brown earth. This past weekend we drove through the rolling countryside of Wisconsin, past farmland itching to get going. I knew this because even in the large field of abandoned fall pumpkins, soggy and mushy from a winter under many inches of snow, I glimpsed green. All along the road there were very few patches of dirty brown snow. It had been replaced by wet soil and the soft new blades of early grass. Overhead countless gaggles of geese danced and undulated in the air, making their way back to old haunts filled with food for starting new families. Still other flocks of birds seemed to be gathering in reunion spots only to lift off high in the air flying in a chaos of black formation.

Down on the lower Mississippi River eagles could be seen standing on the ice floes. In the sky above, their brothers and sisters soared with majesty as if to say, "Look at me! I am your nation's treasured one." I don't think I will ever get accustomed to seeing eagles. At least I hope I won't. The day I cease to be awestruck at the sight of those soaring brown wings, that brilliant white head and tail, will be a sad day indeed. These magnificent birds, once nearly extinct, are also a sign of what happens when we humans rise to our best selves and choose to protect those more vulnerable. As we made changes in our environment that nearly killed these creatures off altogether, so we chose to make changes that would save this symbol of our freedom. Makes you wonder what else we might be capable of, what else might be changed for the common good, doesn't it?

Driving quietly along these roads, truly observing the Earth coming to life again, I thought of the Easter we will soon celebrate. I looked out at what had been dead, frozen ground and glimpsed the life that lay just below its surface. I squinted my eyes and saw the tinge of yellow-green that dances just at the tips of trees that even a few days ago stood cold and barren, sentinels against a gray sky. Even the heavens were edged with life inspiring movement—flapping wings, yellow sunshine and blue sky, a soft breeze that blew away the salt and sand accumulated over winter making room for what is to be born. With my soul eyes, I witnessed the stone being rolled away from the tomb of winter and it made my heart sing an early "Alleluia!"

I know I am getting ahead of myself. March, after all, is the second snowiest month in Minnesota. But the truth is Easter always lives someplace within us and we long for it, must have it. So when we have even a glimmer of its presence we must stand at attention. And standing at attention in this season of Lent and all others is really what it is all about, isn't it? Staying awake to ways in which God shows up in the most unexpected places is our life's work. Giving ourselves over to noticing the daily resurrection moments, not only in the lives of others but in our own life as well, is a holy practice. If Lent teaches us anything it is that, no matter how dark or dreary or despairing things might seem, rebirth is always possible. And that, my friends, is the good news.

So the invitation is to widen your eyes, open your heart and breathe deeply. New Life is on the way!

Practice

Alleluia can be a "churchy" word. But when uttered under your breath or even in your heart it may find power without flash. What new life is brimming around you? No matter the season, new life is nearby someplace. Look for places of new life. Give it an "Alleluia!"

Buiocas Le Dia

At the conclusion of the reading of Isaiah at today's St. Patrick's Day Mass at the Cathedral of St. Paul, we were instructed in how to respond after the reading in Gaelic: *"Buiocas Le Dia." "Thanks be to God."* It has been my practice for the last several years to attend this worship on the Feast Day of St. Patrick, helping remind me and those in attendance that this day is much more than shamrocks and leprechauns. It is the celebration of the life of a real person who took his faith seriously, took giving his life to God seriously. The mass comes complete with bagpipes, of course, and the procession of the Ancient Order of the Hibernians wearing colorful capes and feathery hats while carrying swords, real swords. The service is presided over by the archbishop and all the beauty of a full Roman Catholic mass. The congregation is colorful as well in a multitude of greens and Irish knit sweaters. It is always a high point of the spring for me.

My favorite part of the service comes just before the celebration of the Eucharist as the congregation sings "Anthem for Ireland" words set to the tune of "Danny Boy." This tune alone tugs at the heart strings but the words for this rendition also always bring a little tear to my eye. And I'm not even Irish!

> *O land of love, we bless thee gentle Mother.*
> *O land of light, fair jewel of the sea,*
> *O land of joy, where brother shall meet brother,*
> *And all thy souls shall dwell in harmony.*
> *And when the clouds of torment and of sorrow*
> *Flee with the dark at rising of the sun,*
> *Hand shall clasp hand in happiness tomorrow,*
> *And we shall toil together in God's work begun.*

ANTHEM FOR IRELAND by Nick Haigh/Anita Haigh. Copyright © 2000 Break Of Day Music (Admin. by Song Solutions www.songsolutions.org). Used by permission.

Whether a person is of Irish heritage or not, these are powerful words to sing, to embody. Each of us have been shaped, I believe, by the land where we were born, where we grew up. Whether in the country or the city, near mountains or lakes, rivers or deserts, the land has not only shaped us but also has given us the soil in which to plant our identities. For those who pursue the Holy or are pursued, the land from which we sprang also helps define our understanding of All that is bigger than our human self. The land that shapes us by love, by light, by joy helps us know who we are as workers with God in the unfolding of Creation, helps us "clasp hands" with one another.

In this work, which is our act of living, we can be gifted by an awareness of what it means to be a part of something much larger than house or office, of city or country. It is not a constant awareness, which might be too much for any of us to handle. This awareness comes in glimmers and glimpses and may be accompanied, if we listen well, by music. It might be a tune that sounds a lot like "Danny Boy."

St. Patrick was said to have surrounded himself with words that began: "I arise today through the strength of heaven. . . ." And don't we all? May the strength of heaven guide our feet this day and all those yet to come. *Buiocas Le Dia.*

Practice

Take time today to think of your own ancestry or the land that pulls at your heart. Picture that landscape in your mind and allow it to bless your work and the path. If you have an article of clothing or piece of jewelry that hails from that place, wear it proudly today.

Stray

With the rising of the Sun, let us seek to know God, whose coming is as sure as dawn, whose grace is like rain, renewing the face of the Earth. – HOSEA 6:3

I have been having a crazy-busy week. Everything I have been doing has been wonderful and enlivening. It has just been a whirlwind of meetings, gatherings of people, which has kept me traveling at a certain pace.

As I arrived home yesterday after being in this constant state of motion and as I drove my car into the driveway, my eyes fell on a sweet, little, yellow pansy that had somehow not only survived winter but planted itself in an unlikely place at the edge of our garden. It had taken up the work of shining its yellow face into the world far away from where last year's pansies had been planted. How did it happen, I wondered? Pansies are not perennials but can make their way back in spring in some miraculous and mysterious way. After a year they will bloom not where they were planted, so to speak, but in a space far from their original home.

I don't know how it happened that this little, yellow, spring flower had traveled to where it did. I only know that in the frenzied nature of my week it was the catalyst that caused me to stop, take a deep breath, and remember that I am guest of this world. This sweet little flower was like the hostess of a really great party, saying, "Welcome," with petal-arms held wide, reminding me to take in all the beauty, the change, the gifts of this wonderful world.

And so I did. I walked into the house and put aside the still unfinished to-do list, and I put on my walking shoes and headed out into the waning hours of a beautiful day. As I walked along, I saw so many signs of new life and color being added to a world that has been quickly emerging from its drab state. Crab apple trees are in their full splendor, painting the landscape in pinks and reds. Phlox, purple and white, line sidewalks and rock gardens. Tulips are everywhere—red, yellow, white, purple, orange popping up from the places they have known as home in the frozen ground. I even saw not only dwarf irises, but tall, deep purple irises blooming in a sunny spot along one house. I had probably ridden by many similar scenes during the day, scenes that had gone unnoticed traveling at my own version of warp speed.

And yet this stray, yellow pansy had been the swift kick that woke me up, that reminded me that this living is a blessing. Without its far-flung presence I might have walked into the house, opened my computer, and continued chipping away at my perceived important list, doing what I thought "needed" to be done. Instead this little flower provided a much needed time out, not sitting in a chair until I learned to behave, but heading out into the world to be dazzled. It seems the Universe had other plans for me, and I needed a wake up call.

For all those strays—those planted in places that seem irregular, unplanned, misplaced—I give thanks. They just might be in that place for a reason beyond their knowing, waiting to give guidance to a pilgrim who has lost the way.

Practice

Make a point of keeping your eyes wide open this day. Remember to look in the unlikely places for signs of wonder. When the dazzling arrives, offer your gratitude.

A Thin Place

"Thin places," the Celts call this space,
Both seen and unseen,
Where the door between the world
And the next is cracked open for a moment
And the light is not all on the other side.
God shaped space. Holy. – SHARLANDE SLEDGE

In the Celtic Christian tradition there is the concept of a thin place—a luminous experience in which one senses the veil between the earthly world, what can be seen and touched, and the eternal is thin, permeable even. If you read Celtic authors at all, it won't be long until this concept creeps into the writing. It is most visible in our understanding of the "great cloud of witnesses." Particularly in the scriptures you may hear it in the season of Easter or near the end of October when Halloween and All Saints' Day arrives. It is in these readings that we hear of the disciples' experience of the "showings" of Jesus after his death and resurrection. During that week, for instance, we read about Jesus appearing to the disciples when they are not having much luck in their chosen line of work, fishing. After they see him, their nets are full to overflowing. It is a rich and fascinating story that has endless facets to discover.

This week I am having my own thin place experience. It has happened right around this time for the last few years. In our front yard stands a cherry bush, about four feet in height. Right now it is covered with delicate little pink blossoms. Like most every other blooming plant, it is a week or so ahead of schedule given the weather and early spring we've experienced. The bush was a gift from my dearest friends, my book club, to honor and remember my father who died on April 23 several years ago. Since the bush's planting it has bloomed every year on and around the anniversary of his death and has provided me with an unexplainable experience of him. Since the first sighting of the blossoms, I have now watched and waited for another showing, another thin place, that allows the present and the eternal to meld. During these days I think of him more often, his sweet, gentle way much like the pink blossoms on the bush, and, of course, his love of cherry pie.

A couple of years ago I shared this story with my mother who told my brothers, and now they also want to hear the progress of the cherry bush. " Is it blooming yet?" they ask when they call. I give an update on the status of the bush, and we all are pulled into the deep longing and symbolism this bush now represents. My mother has now shared the bush story with my eight-year-old nephew. Not long ago he asked if the bush would be blooming soon. He remarked that somehow "Poppy knows" about the bush. "I wish I could see it," he said. The experience of the thin place has now been passed on to another generation.

The stories of Jesus' appearances to the disciples after his death carry so much: comfort, validation, affirmation, encouragement, hope, fulfillment. Over the years as these accounts have been retold, they have taken on deeper and richer meanings. Our post-Enlightenment minds ask questions about the "truth" of the stories. Did he really appear, or did they imagine it? Did their luck improve because they saw Jesus, or was it just the movement of the undercurrents that brought the fish to the net? Or was their experience of the one they loved so full, so deep, so rich, that they were enveloped in the veil that exists between the worlds, a veil we cannot hope to understand but must accept as pure Mystery?

I am going for the Mystery. I am claiming the gift of not knowing. Whether it's fish stories or blooming bushes, I place my faith in the thin place that exists between what I cannot see and what I pray is present. I will continue to watch the cherry bush and feel the closeness I long for, the person I miss. And I will continue to tell the story just as the disciples did.

It simply seems like the right thing to do.

Practice

Have you experienced a thin place? Have you had a time when the veil between this world and the other seems to be permeable? Name those times. Honor them. Stand in the Mystery.

Coexist

"A bird doesn't sing because it has an answer. It sings because it has a song."
— MAYA ANGELOU

I have had the privilege of spending the last several days in northern Wisconsin watching spring arrive. When we showed up on beautiful Papoose Lake, the temperatures were warm and the water was like glass. There was no sign of the boats that can dot this little lake in the middle of summer. Not long after arriving, my husband hung a bird feeder off the deck and filled it with seed. By the time we had unpacked clothes and the groceries had filled the refrigerator with the staples that would sustain us for the next several days, birds of all kinds had begun showing up. How did they know? How did they know there was a new food source in the neighborhood? Do birds have a signal, a certain call, that says "soup's on!"?

The first to arrive were the gold finches. Like the best dressed girls at the prom, their brilliant yellow feathers created nearly the only dash of color in the still leafless landscape. They were soon followed by chickadees with their sweet little gray and black bodies, their tiny beaks pecking away at the feeder. A glance away to make a cup of coffee was followed by the appearance of house finches, their red and orangish feathers seeming more intense than when they are seen in midsummer. Not long after, the message must have arrived to the nuthatches, and they came to share in the discovered bounty. At one point I looked out and there was a different kind of bird on every perch of the feeder, all eating quietly, obviously right at home with the diversity at their dinner table. By day's end a few starlings had also shown up only to find it difficult, though not impossible, to poke their large beaks into the feeding holes. They seemed content with eating the "leftovers" the other birds had knocked to the ground below.

Watching this movable feast, I was reminded of the bumper sticker I see with great regularity as I make my way on Minnesota highways. Using the primary symbols

of many faith traditions, the symbols are aligned to spell the word "COEXIST." Tacked to the back of various cars, it carries the deep hope that the people of the world and our nation will find ways to see the common ways we can live together as people of faith. Though our words might be different, our emphases divergent, the ways we speak of the Holy diverse, the hope of being able to coexist with respect and an appreciation for those whose faith and life experience is different from our own is, I believe, a noble and important goal. As I watched these beautiful and fragile little creatures coexist at the same feeder, my heart was warmed by their willingness to feast from the same table, and I sent a prayer that those of us without wings might learn to do the same.

In four days, these lovely winged ones had gone through nearly two fillings of the feeder. As the days warmed and the sun became more intense, the birch trees began to show a glimmer of yellow green at their tops. The grass that is planted in places by those who want to mow while they are "at the lake" had grown and turned a deep green. I even saw one homeowner out tackling his first mow of the year. From a human perspective, four days of recreation allowed for relaxed muscles, deep rest, and some good reading time. I am sure that those who saw me today were unable to see the kind of marked difference in me that I witnessed in the changes of nature. Growth happened all around me. Newness came to the landscape. And the birds provided a powerful lesson.

And so today I will begin once again my endeavor to COEXIST after the example of my feathered friends.

Practice

Search out a phrase of wisdom or prayer from another tradition. Carry it with you and allow it to inform your own expression of faith.

Earth Day

The message of Genesis is not domination but appreciation. We, who the text says are made in God's image, ought to reflect God's attitude toward nature: appreciation. — SALLIE McFAGUE

In case no one has said this to you today: "Happy Earth Day!" I have now been offered this greeting by a couple of people, accompanied by huge smiles. I also received this greeting by email with the still breathtaking image of the Earth from space. I never seem to tire of seeing it. Perhaps it is the memory of that first time I saw it and the realization that I was seeing the fullness of my home as it floated in the greater universe. There was the feeling of both total awe and the recognition of the tiny speck that I am in comparison. Though I have seen it countless times since, I find my reaction is still tinged with that original wonder.

It seems impossible to me that we are celebrating the fortieth anniversary of Earth Day. I recall the first one in 1970 and the excitement I felt that so many people were uniting to speak on behalf of our troubled environment. As a high school aged kid, it seeded some hope in me for the ways people, working in solidarity, can make a difference in the world. And over the years, though there have been setbacks and challenges, there have also been increased care for our world that has saved species, cleaned up lakes and rivers, called a halt to those things that pollute our air, and generally changed the ways we are aware of our human impact on our environment. There is still much to do to stop the effects of global climate change and yet we now know more than we ever have about what needs to change, what needs our attention, what ways we must continue to stand in solidarity.

For me, Earth Day has always been an extension of how I have understood my life in faith. For reasons unclear to me, my central experience of the Holy has

always been grounded in the goodness of Creation. While I am sure these were not the messages spoken from the pulpit of my childhood, messages most often filled with a violent, angry, punitive image of God, I somehow walked into adolescence and adulthood with an image of a Creator God. This Creator moved through all of Creation, not just the human ones, but all—trees, water, air, animals, birds, insects, all—and continues to bring birth in ways that seem unimaginable. It has brought a reverence for life to my way of walking in the world for which I am grateful.

While I was in seminary I read one of Sallie McFague's books called *The Body of God*. McFague, whose words are quoted above, used the image of the Earth as not a mere metaphor for God but as an example of how we experience the Holy. The Earth, she pointed out, was how we truly experience how God works in the world and to harm the Earth is to harm God. I remember finding it a challenging and yet inspiring book which challenged my understanding of God's presence. It also gave new meaning to what it meant to be an environmentalist.

Earth Day has seemed to extend even further into more than just one day. People have been celebrating all week. We will have a special Earth Day worship service on Sunday, and I know other churches scheduled one also. In our service we will read the sacred texts that speak of Creator and Creation and our amazing interdependence. We will be reminded that in the scriptures Earth Day was not just one day but every day. We hear it in Genesis, the Psalms, in Ezekiel and Job and the other prophets, and in the many stories Jesus tells to instruct the people of what it means to reside in the "kingdom" of God. His stories of fishermen and farmers, bakers and healers, all tell of those who are deeply grounded in what it means to be people of the Earth.

On this blessed Earth Day, may we find ourselves at day's end filled with appreciation, deep appreciation for the gifts of this spinning planet we call home— sweet home. And may we carry that appreciation forward into the next day and the next and the next.

Practice

How do you see God's movement in Creation? What are you noticing about the unfolding earth around you? Find one scene in the landscape you travel each day. Offer a prayer for its continued growth and health.

Same Old, Same Old

Using the same old materials of earth, air, fire, and water, every twenty-four hours God creates something new out of them. If you think you're seeing the same show all over again seven times a week, you're crazy. Every morning you wake up to something that in all eternity never was before and never will be again. And the you that wakes up was never the same before and will never be the same again either.
– FREDERICK BUECHNER

Last night I was driving in my car minding my own business when…boom…there was the Sun as fire-red brilliant as I have ever seen it. It was setting in the west, and I happened to be driving past a beautifully groomed golf course, the grass a luscious green, providing a stage for this Hollywood-style ending to a day. I strained my ears to listen for whatever sun-setting music must be playing somewhere. No music. Just the pulsing colors of fire filling the sky. It was a "Wow!" moment stuck right in the middle of my week.

Certainly I have seen amazing sunsets before, but this one seemed somehow special. Maybe it wasn't the sunset at all that was different. Maybe it was me. Perhaps whatever had happened in my day had created the perfect soil for me to be able to see the beauty of the setting sun in a new way, with new eyes, sacred eyes. Whatever it was, I knew that the ending to this April day was anything but same old, same old.

If we give ourselves room to really think about the experience of our living we might come to the same realization as Frederick Buechner did. When I read his words, I was reminded how, sometimes, as we begin our worship on a Sunday morning, I remind those gathered that there has never been a moment like the one we are sharing. The people there have never been together before. Though most know one another well, there are always a few guests who cause us to be something different than we were only a few hours earlier when we raised our heads from our pillows. The circle that has gathered has never been before and will not be again. Fascinating to think about, isn't it?

What if we took this realization seriously? What if we approached each morning, each day, for the fresh start it truly is? What if we opened our eyes ready to step out in a new way, filled with the hope of what we might bring to the world that has never been brought before? I find this prospect exhilarating. Do you? Somehow it seems to me that it connects us with the fragility and the blessing of our living. We are called to be creators and co-creators with the Holy using, perhaps, the same old materials, but in anything but the same old ways. Every day. And not one of our days can be repeated in the exact same way. Each one is a unique experience.

And if that is the case, it seems the only real way to live is to savor them all.

Practice

Make a point of observing both the rising and the setting of the sun. Note the fullness that has happened in the hours between. Give thanks for the gift of the day.

Grace Please

Grant me the grace this day
to rest and remember
that there is nothing I have to do,
nothing I have to buy or sell,
nothing I have to produce or consume
in order to become who I already am:
your beloved creation.

    May your overworked creation
    and those who cannot rest today
    come to know the liberation of your sabbath. – SAM HAMILTON-POORE

I have had one of those warp speed weeks, and it is only Wednesday! I seem to have checked things off my to-do list as fast as I can add yet another urgent matter. Honesty requires that I say that everything I have been doing has been wonderful, a blessing. The stars have simply aligned to allow for several creation projects all at one time. Some weeks seem to have more than their share, don't they?

One of the blessings that has been mine this week is to be a part of a team that is planning a worship service for the fortieth anniversary celebration of Earth Day. How can it be forty years since we first honored this day set aside to remember and re-affirm our responsibility as humans living on this amazing Creation? While looking through some worship resources, I found the prayer that is printed above. I thought it was lovely and captured where I believe many people find themselves. I know I certainly do. How many times I measure my worth by what I feel I "must" produce, what I feel I "should" do, what I think I "need" to buy in order to be a whole person. This spiral almost always leads me farther from who I truly am: a

Poem used by permission of Sam Hamilton-Poore.

beloved creation of God, full and complete just as I am. The same, I believe, can be said of all human beings.

The practice of sabbath holds a very important purpose: to stop us in our tracks long enough for us to remember who we are. Whether overworked or unable to rest, a practice of calling a halt to the frenetic activity most of us cave in to and feel is demanded of us, allows our body, mind and spirit to breathe deeply of the One who carries us even when we fail to notice. As the prayer suggests, there is liberation in that.

Sabbath moments can encompass full days, an hour here and there, or simply an intentional sipping of a cup of tea. These spring days provide the perfect setting for moments of sabbath. Noticing, really observing the emerging tulip blooms in the yards we pass, how they slowly open like the wings of a butterfly. Allowing the time to check in every day with the maple tree that is doing its work of producing leaves for summer shade, watching how each day there is a minute amount of growth to be seen. Looking down at the sidewalk, keeping an eye out for the mounds of ants that have returned and can be seen crawling over one another doing who knows what and stopping to see if you can allow your eye to track just one particular insect as it zooms within a two- to three-inch radius. All are possible moments of liberation, of remembering who we are—observers, fellow earth travelers, historians, poets, storytellers, psalmists.

Today is as good a day as any to take a break, to begin the practice of sabbath moments. Today is as good a day as any to reach for liberation, the liberation of remembering who we are and for offering our gratitude to the One who called us into being. Today is as good a day as any to ask for grace, please?

Practice

Give yourself the gift of a sabbath moment . . . or hour . . . or day. Remember who you are and give thanks.

Meditation

This morning I was privileged to observe a small turtle that had made its way out of a pond that skirts a walking path I frequent. I watched as it sat in the morning sun, the dewy grass creating a cool nest and also a sense of camouflaged safety. Its dark green shell and its lighter green head blended in quite nicely among the blades of newly mowed grass. My eye had only caught the sight of it because it was reaching its head upward, and I saw the movement of the breath in the length of its neck. I stopped for quite some time, watching its breath go in and out, in and out. Its contentment was contagious as I observed it and found myself aware of my own breath, in and out, in and out. The turtle and I were breathing together.

I do not know in what tradition or context meditation first was practiced. But if I were to speculate, I would say that someone observed the pace and rhythm of a turtle and knew that somehow their way of moving in the world was a good thing. I could imagine that first one human practiced the rhythm of movement and breath employed by this slow, moving one who carried its house with it. I have thought about this creature all day, wondering if it is still sitting in the beautiful place it was this morning. The dew might have evaporated all around it and the sun might have risen higher in the sky. But the turtle was in a good place, a happy place and so why move on? Somehow I think there is much to be learned from this languid creature.

As I walked away from my turtle encounter I made my way along streets that are being resurfaced in our neighborhood. I was forced to the side of the road by an enormous, earth moving piece of construction equipment as it crept along the street. This large piece of machinery and the small turtle, though drastically different in appearance, had something in common—a lack of speed. These two encounters gave shape to my day. Instead of speeding from one thing to the next, I found myself taking the time that was needed in each meeting, each conversation. I have allowed myself to be fully present to the moment at hand, moving with the rhythm of the turtle or the earth mover. And I have found that no work was neglected in this endeavor. Imagine that.

Gandhi was reported to have said, *"There is more to life than increasing its speed."* Today I am thankful to the lovely little turtle who halted the hare in me and allowed me to be completely present to the beauty of this day. What a blessing it has been!

Practice

Do something slowly today. Find the rhythm of your breath. Stay with it and allow it to slow down and take your body with it. Eat slowly. Walk slowly. Answer questions or phones slowly. Notice how this slowing down makes you feel.

Goodness

The grace of the love of the skies be thine,
The grace of the love of the stars be thine,
The grace of the love of the moon be thine,
The grace of the love of the sun be thine.
– CARMINA GADELICA

Over the last couple of days I have been rereading J. Philip Newell's lovely little book, *Listening to the Heartbeat of God*. This book uses many prayers from the early Celts which have been collected in a book called *Carmina Gadelica* which simply means "songs and poems of the Gaels." It is a collection of the unceasing prayers of people of the Scottish Hebrides, those tied closely to the earth, who understood the Holy's movement in their lives. This was true in the day-to-day tasks of laying a fire that would warm their home and cook their food, in the birth and death of their animals, family, and neighbors. The prayers reflect that they saw no part of their life in which God was not active. They are beautiful, sweet, sometimes simple prayers passed down orally to generation after generation until they were finally collected by Alexander Carmichael in the late nineteenth century.

I thought yesterday about how far we have moved from this kind of deep understanding of our connection with Creator and creation. I wonder how many people say a prayer as they turn the gas on to warm the teapot that will create the hot water for their morning cup. I know I certainly don't. With a turn of the knob I watch fire flare forth and turn toward the next thing to be done, never giving a single thought to the gift of this amazing source of warmth. I wonder how many people took the tiny plants that have been planted in gardens over the last several days, held them gently, saying a prayer for the wonder of seed that sprouts into food to nourish our bodies. How many of us pass by fields full of dairy cows and raise our hands in blessing for the milk that builds our bones and brings us the pleasure of ice cream on a warm summer's day? So many things to be thankful over. . . .

There is a kind of envy that wells up in me when I think of these early faithful giving thanks for the ways they were connected to their God. And yet nothing except intention and a perception of busyness keeps me from following their lead. Yesterday I told a coworker that it seemed nearly a sin to have left my backyard to go any place else. The bold purple irises were so splendid. The columbine, lavender and dainty, had just bloomed. The bright red gerbera daisies were lifting their faces toward the sunlight. I could have spent the whole day moving from plant to plant, enveloped in the awe of it. But somehow duty called and I answered.

And if the beauty and wonder of these earth-bound ones weren't enough, what about that moon last night? The deep blue night of sky was hung with a yellow moon so bright it must have kept the most sensitive awake with its brilliance. As I crossed the bridge over the Mississippi coming home from a late night meeting, I saw it hanging in the sky like a huge dinner plate waiting to be feasted upon. The ancient Celtic cells in my body collected into a prayer with no words, only deep breath, and an even deeper connection to something I can only describe as Sacred.

Perhaps it is romantic to think that, in the twenty-first century, we might be as prayerful as those in earlier times. Perhaps it is not possible to connect our daily actions with the Holy as deeply as they did. But I do believe that living with a sense of humility about our place in the family of things cannot be a bad thing. The beauty of the iris, the majesty of last night's moon, was something I had no hand in creating. And yet it was a gift to me from a Source bigger than I can imagine. And for that I offer my praise and my gratitude. Amen.

Practice

To what part of Creation might you be intentionally connected today? In what part of your life might you be intentionally aware of the Holy's movement? Allow this to be your practice.

Beauty and Brevity

I often thing of the heavens
    your hands have made,
    and of the moon and stars
    you put in place.
Then I ask, "Why do you care
    about us humans"
    Why are you concerned
    for us weaklings?"
You made us a little lower
    than you did yourself.
    and you have crowned us
    with glory and honor.
– PSALM 8:3-5

Pay attention, my children!
    Follow my advice,
    and you will be happy.
Listen carefully
    to my instructions,
    and you will be wise.
Come to my home each day
    and listen to me.
    You will find happiness.
By finding me, you find life,
    and the Holy will be pleased with you.
– PROVERBS 8:32-35

Yesterday we were surrounded by these two "pieces of 8" in our worship. Both

Proverbs 8 and Psalm 8 speak of the beauty and fragility of the created world. I commend them to you in their entirety. Proversb speaks of our search for wisdom among the gifts of Creation while the psalmist lauds God's work in Creation, asking what the human purpose is in the midst of it all.

These two scriptures created a kind of perfect storm of words to bless my experience of yesterday. It was, in truth, a nearly perfect summer day. Warm and sunny with a marvelous rain storm that came in late afternoon. The brilliance of all that is blooming—trees, flowers, plants—created a palette of color that dazzled the eye. Outside the entrance to our church, pink and red shrub roses line the walkways and a labyrinth, creating a welcome of both sight and sweet scent. The rain not only cooled things and gave a free watering to plants fresh to the ground but also brought about an end to those flowers which had been lingering past their spring prime. What had looked bright and beautiful in the morning seemed a little aged and worn by day's end.

If we are awake to the daily movement of the season's work, we can honor this brevity of beauty, the elusive nature of it all. It is, I believe, an important life lesson to learn that a rose will not always be as beautiful as it is in the first days of blooming. The same may, of course, be said of so much of our living. The sweetness of an infant, the precocious nature of a three year old, the poignant longing of an adolescent, the wide-eyed wonder of someone newly in love—all change and come to some kind of end. So the ability to be present to the fullness of miracle in each day, in each stage, is something to practice.

The invitation is ours each morning to awake with the blank slate of the every day looming before us. As our eyes open, and I dare say our hearts as well, we can come to know the fullness that is this life, which is pure gift. This day can never be repeated so, perhaps, it would serve each of us well to consider wisely what we choose to do with it, how we will choose to hold its precious minutes and hours.

The beauty, the fullness, the goodness awaits. Are you ready?

Practice

Choose well what you will do with this day. On a small piece of paper jot down one or two things you want to do to celebrate the fact that you are alive. Keep it near you as a reminder.

Transitions

For everything there is a season. . . . – ECCLESIASTES 3

Being one of those people who often talk their way into an understanding of personal awareness, I found myself explaining to a group of dear friends yesterday what was going on in my life. As I talked my way through it, I realized that I am in the presence of many transitions. I am surrounded by people and situations that are experiencing in-between times. I was reminded of a conversation I had a couple of years ago with explorer Anne Bancroft who described herself as "between expeditions." The metaphor has stuck with me. Her words rang true to me yesterday as I talked my way into a deep understanding.

Many people I know are in transition. Some are on the verge of retirement, while others have just graduated from college and have their whole career ahead of them. Some are unemployed and filled with soul searching that is laced with anxiety and fear. Still others are in the midst of jobs that are taking on new shapes that cause challenges and opportunities. Most institutions, including the church where I have a life, are also in a time of great transition: not what and who they were, not yet what they will become. Transition is all around.

As I took a morning walk, I was also aware of all the transition around me. The evidence of the work in people's gardens and yards was everywhere to be seen. Upturned soil housed newly-planted vegetables and flowers. Shovels leaned against the sides of houses. Piles of uprooted plants sat in buckets to be thrown or replanted or given away. All the human hands at work had participated in creating a visual image of transition. None of these garden plots will look the same in a few short weeks. Some of the plans for how the garden will succeed, no doubt plotted in the dead of winter's cold, will flourish and grow. There will also be surprises, unplanned gifts that the gardener could not have expected. And only part of the

success of the garden can be claimed by the ones who did the planting. Forces greater than those with dirty knees and sore muscles are also a part of this great Creation. Weather, sun, rain, stray animals, insects all contribute to what grows and what doesn't.

And so it is with all transitions. We hold only a piece of the great puzzle that will eventually take us from one place in the journey to the next. But there are so many other, unseen, pieces that take our trust, our faith, our sitting still. Trusting that there is much to be learned in the in-between place can make all the difference. The tomato plant in May is only a few green leaves on a stem. Come August the red, ripe, juicy fruit will bring delight beyond measure.

For the in-between times, it is a good image to remember.

Practice

Take stock of what transitions are around you. Create a ritual for honoring this transition and your feelings about it. Tell someone about it.

Paying Homage

This morning started out with a flurry of activity. Last night I had baked a cake that I wanted to share with my co-workers and knew I had to run to the grocery store this morning for whipping cream to top it off. My feet hit the floor with the running list of "to be done" zooming through my head. Making my way downstairs I found that we, in the night, had been home to a sick dog in the living room. (You don't want to know.) This threw a wrench into the works of what was already an out-of-the-ordinary morning. By the time breakfast was eaten, hair was washed, dishwasher loaded, lunch packed, paper read, I felt as if I had lived nearly a full day and it wasn't even 8:00 a.m. Several times in my bustling about I had glimpsed, out the window, the grape iris in our garden as it seemed to grow even taller, reaching toward the sun. Each time I saw it I thought, "I have to go out there and look, really look at it." Distracted by the next thing, I moved on and never made it outside.

As the morning sun shone on the backyard, its rays coaxed the brilliant purple petals open on this queen of the garden. I busily packed all the stuff I needed for my day into my car and backed out of the driveway. As I buckled my seat belt, my eyes caught one last view of the stately iris. I made it all the way out of the driveway and several feet down the street. Then I stopped. I halted the busyness of the morning and pulled over and parked my car. With purpose, I got out and walked back up the driveway and into the backyard to do the one thing I truly should have done all morning. I walked up and stood looking at the sun's rays falling across the deep purple of the iris. I stared into the heart of it, its deep yellow center with the brown stripes like eyebrows floating out toward the petal edges. (How is this possible?) The sun caught the colors as I reached down to smell the grape scent that emits from the deep purple, a smell that only comes my way for a few days of every year of my life. In just a matter of weeks these beautiful flowers will have died and been cut back as the next wave of color arrives in the garden. To have missed it would have been, dare I say it, sinful.

This morning was for paying homage, for being a pilgrim in my own backyard. I could have missed it. I could have continued driving and made my way onto the freeway and the rest of my day. But something inside me would not let me go; it urged me to stop and see. Whether is was the Spirit or just good common sense depends on your perspective, I suppose. Whatever it was, I am grateful for it. It has made all the difference in this day.

> *Each day, every moment, you place your hand of blessing upon the brow of creation. In your touch, in your words, everything flowers, everything remembers the deep, perfect loveliness within. The deep, perfect loveliness of you.*
> – SAM HAMILTON-POORE, *Earth Gospel*

Practice

What sight is drawing you? Give into it. Spend time, precious time, looking with your deepest heart. Offer a prayer of gratitude for the gift of seeing and the blessing of paying attention.

Quote used by permission of Sam Hamilton-Poore.

Mulling

We are aware that all generations of our ancestors and all future generations are present in us. – THICH NHAT HANH

Today could have been called "Mulling Monday." I have been mulling over a statement made yesterday by a photographer who was sharing his images and his own spirituality and theology with those of us who are seeking to open our eyes to the presence of the Holy. His images were stunning, funny, poignant, breathtaking. How he was able to be so fluidly articulate in his understanding of the Sacred showed not only his ability to integrate his life, but also the depth of the work he had done to get to this place of wisdom. All this was accompanied by amazing photography. He was someone known by many in the community, and so his ability to connect with his audience was sincere and simple.

At one point he was showing an image of a great gray owl peeking from behind a tree trunk, its yellow eye staring straight at the camera. At first glance it was difficult to see where tree ended and bird began. Everyone was staring intently at the photograph when he said: "We do not see with our eyes. We really see with our brains. That means that many of you are in this picture also. All we have experienced together is stored in my brain and becomes a part of the lens with which I saw this image."

Can you understand why I have been mulling this idea over all day? Since I am not a scientist and he is, I have to take the science of it all on his word. But it makes sense to me. I can think of all the people who have come and gone from my life who have shaped the lens with which I see the world. Those who have shown me compassion in difficult times and have helped me see the generous thread that makes its way in the blood and bone of all humans. Those who have been playful, who have made me laugh and who have needled me out of my intensity to be able

to see the truly silly and frivolous that exists in so many unexpected places. Those who have given me the benefit of the doubt when I perhaps did not deserve it and taught me the gift of grace. So many messages planted deep in my brain by countless people giving me my own unique lens.

The intention of the talk was to have helped people take better nature photography. But the message we all received was so much bigger than any camera or picture we might ever take. The message was really a call to see the deep connections we have with one another even when we are unaware—and the equally deep connections we make each time we form a relationship with another human, an animal, a landscape. All these relationships form a matrix in our brain giving us a world view that is unlike any other. If we are lucky we will remember this every now and then and give thanks as we try to think who is helping us see the moment.

I'm afraid Mulling Monday may ooze into Mulling Tuesday and Wednesday and on and on. It's a lot to take in, and my brain feels pretty small. Small, maybe. But very, very full.

Practice

On a small piece of paper, create a web of lines. Begin to name all those who have helped you form the connections with which you see the world. Speak their names into the world and allow the gift of their presence to wash your day.

Hush!

If you were awake this morning at 6:28 a.m. you could have welcomed the beginning of summer. Today we will experience the day of longest light and the night of shortest darkness. For years this was something that went unnoticed to me. But now that the marking of this day has become a part of my yearly celebrations. I wonder at how this honoring slipped out of favor with, not only people of faith, but the majority of people in general. It is clear that for several hundreds of years, a celebration of the longest day and longest night, summer and winter solstice, was something that was important to people. It was how they knew that life was continuing and that their God was at work. This was true especially to those who lived further from the equator where the extremes of light and darkness are so pronounced. Since the metaphors of light and darkness are so prevalent in the scriptures, it seems logical to me that marking these turning points of the year would be important.

Today, like all days, is an opportunity to celebrate the mysterious and awe-producing ways our Creator God moves in the world, bringing the sad laments of stark winter out of the grave and into the arms of teeming summer. Often we must rely on the poets, the songwriters, or the storytellers to help us give language to this experience. And yet, how could we, how should we, miss the opportunity for praise at such a magnificent wonder? Those who once lived closer to the rhythms of the earth knew something we, in our concrete jungles and technological lifestyles, have forgotten: This world is a magnificent on-going creation of which we are only a small part.

But make no mistake, our part is very important. We are the witnesses. We are the ones who tell the stories and prepare the next generation of storytellers and dreamers. If we take our role seriously, we can recapture the habit of stopping our

spinning lifestyles long enough to notice the seasons changing, the play of light on the shadows we cast on this longest day. We can say our prayers quickly and intentionally on this shortest of all nights.

Hush! Listen! The world is alive!

Practice

Spend at least ten minutes today listening. Turn off all the knobs and buttons that might lure you and simply listen to the world around. What do you hear? What have you been missing?

Hungry and Thirsty

As a mother shall she meet him. . . .
With the Bread of Understanding
* shall she feed him,*
And give him the Water of Wisdom
* to drink.* – WISDOM OF JESUS BEN SIRACH 15:2-3

I read an article this morning in the newspaper about a man who will be running Grandma's Marathon in Duluth this weekend. The article tells of his loss of 145 pounds, his being in recovery from alcoholism, and his training and work toward this incredible feat of running a marathon after years of abusing his body, mind, and spirit. It was an inspiring story of someone who was searching for what could feed him, what could quench a deep thirst that eluded him. While his story is one of extremes of both tragedy and triumph, I believe we all carry a little of his story within us. We are, each of us, hungry and thirsty for something that can often seem just outside our reach. We can go through all manner of things to satisfy that longing; some that are helpful and healthy and others that temporarily fill an empty spot at our center with what makes us feel good but does not touch the depth of what resides within.

We carry within us hunger and thirst for something. What do you long for? What gnaws at your stomach in the middle of the night, aching to be filled? These words from the Wisdom texts of the Bible, that section that rests between the Older Testament and the Christian scriptures, hint at what, I believe, we all long for. Understanding. Wisdom. At our core we all want to be known and understood. By our families, our friends, our co-workers. Understood for what makes us tick, what we love, what we hope for, where we see ourselves in the big picture of the world. And we all want to grow into wisdom. Wisdom to know our place in the universe, what our gifts are and how we are meant to share them, who we are and why we are here. If we are lucky we have had parents, grandparents, teachers, and mentors

who have helped us ask ourselves these questions in safe and healthy ways. They have stood by us as we faltered, until we have discovered our way to a place of understanding and wisdom. I pray that has been the case for you.

And yet, we also know those who have not had this kind of nest in which to land, grow, mature. We can read the stories of those people in the newspaper every day. Those who search in all the wrong places for the bread of understanding and the water of wisdom, but find themselves in deep, dark waters, often drowning in lives of pain and despair. Perhaps you know someone like this. Perhaps you are struggling in just this way right now.

This weekend we will celebrate Father's Day, a day when we honor the men who raised, shaped, and inspired us. I recognize that not everyone's experience of their father is a happy one and that this day can have its own set of complications. Others have much to celebrate as they honor or remember fathers who have shared love, laughter, and lessons that are full of joy. But each of us, whether male or female, mother or father, has the potential to offer the bread of understanding and the water of wisdom to those we meet, particularly those we know are struggling to fill a deep longing that may be unnameable to them. Being a parent is not only biological but is also about circumstance and proximity. We can all be parent and mentor. And that is something to celebrate.

Sometimes life can seem like a marathon, a race that can tax our energy, resources, and our very souls. But how much more beautiful it all becomes when we know that there is someone out ahead cheering us on, meeting us with understanding, offering the wisdom of their experience. Whether on the giving or receiving end, everyone becomes a winner.

Practice

Take time to remember and name those who have nurtured your path. Reach out to someone you know who is struggling. Offer your prayers for both mentor and searcher.

Two Shoes

Christ wears "two shoes" in the world: Scripture and nature. Both are necessary to understand the Lord, and at no stage can creation be seen as a separation of things from God. – JOHN SCOTUS ERIUGENA (810-77)

I came across this wise man in reading John Philip Newell's books, *Christ of the Celts* and *Listening to the Heartbeat of God*. Eriugena was an Irish theologian, philosopher, and poet known as one of the wisest and most read in the Middle Ages. He was thought by some, but not all, to have strayed from orthodox Christian teachings as he wrote about how the entire Creation—all people, animals, beings—reflect some attributes of God. He saw a day when all creatures would live in harmony with God. He based his beliefs on the Greek writings of the early Christians. And, unlike some others, he lived to tell the tale!

Once while our community was living into the theme of "Open My Eyes," I thought about good old Eriugena. To think that more than 1200 years ago someone talked about Christ's two shoes—scripture and creation—astounds me. I think of the many circles today where this statement could still get you booted out the door. And I am thankful to be in a faith community where this is not the case.

And yet, who can not look at the unfolding seasons around us and not see the movement of something larger than the human creatures? It is spring. I have a sweet bouquet of pansies sitting on my desk, smiling back at me. This gift from a friend has brightened my stress-filled day, bringing a certain salvation of color and simplicity that was needed. As I look outside, I see the mighty oak tree towering outside my window. Each season I learn as much about resurrection from this tree's bare branches, buds, and leaves as I do from the gospels. It is true I would not have the fullness of God without one or the other. Like Christ, I need both shoes to give word and work to God's movement in my life.

I do not believe this is just a church camp way of theology, a feel good sentiment. When I wear both shoes, I am firmly planted in the world in which God still speaks over and over again. The scriptures help me interpret how Creation invites me to give shape to faith in my time and place. It is a lovely, sometimes confusing, always transforming dance. The music changes with the seasons of both age and climate. But the partner, the Great Artist, keeps inviting.

May I have this dance?

Practice

Spend time today with your favorite scripture or sacred text. Take these words outside and into the world. How does the shoe of creation and these words dance together? Do you see something new in either or both?

Blueberry Prayers

On Friday I had the blessing of being invited to pick blueberries with close friends. The invitation included a beautiful drive south, through the hills and bluffs of Minnesota's river valley along the shores of the Mississippi and through the corn and soybean fields that are the lifeblood of farm families. The whole trip was a testament to the gifts of beauty and of summer. As we curved and jogged off the main highway toward the berry farm, farmhouses and animals—cows, horses, ponies, even a sweet, little donkey—seemed to greet the city dwellers. "Welcome to our world! Come and rest awhile!" they seemed to say.

Upon our arrival, we saw that we were not the only people who woke up and thought that picking blueberries was the thing to do this day. Cars lined the makeshift parking lot that, in the winter, must be nothing more than the entrance to the barn and the side yard. Children played on a tire swing hung from a huge oak tree nestled in the backyard of the farmhouse. "Why did they put a swing here?" I heard one city boy ask. What better place for a swing, I thought, as I took in the view of the green, rolling hills. Swinging from that tree must feel like flying!

As we approached the blueberry fields, I noticed three different places where Buddhist prayer flags flew in the early morning breeze. The flags, tied to stakes in the ground, formed a canopy to the entrance of the fields and ringed the shelter where our berries would eventually be weighed and priced. The flags' bright primary colors—red, yellow, blue, green and white—were now faded from the sun and frayed from the wind. But they still held a peaceful, steady presence over the berries and the hands who picked the luscious, blue fruit. I wondered what prayers had been infused in those pieces of fabric, prayers for a good crop, for sunshine, for rain, for temperatures that made for a bountiful harvest. All, prayers of hope.

If you pick alone, the act of picking berries allows for quiet time, for noticing your own breath, the sweat that forms at your temples and the nape of your neck. It can become a meditative time. It also allows for over hearing the conversations of those around you. Two women one row over lamented the aches and pains of growing older. Their conversation was punctuated with laughter directed at themselves. A family on my other side talked about the games they were playing with guests at their home. "Can you play that game in French?" the mother asked. The sound of young voices speaking French followed. Amazing!

But perhaps the best words I heard came at the height of my picking. A new crop of pickers arrived and, as they made their way into the field, one young girl could not contain herself. "Look! Look! It's a blueberry wonderland!"

And indeed it was. A blueberry wonderland created through hard work and, no doubt, sacrifice, held in the gentle breeze by good weather, ripe conditions, countless prayers, and a life based in hope.

Practice

Pay attention to the food you eat this day. Take time to imagine its path to your table. Give thanks for the hands that planted and harvested it. Taste its flavor and give thanks.

Last Child in the Woods

Those who contemplate the beauty of the earth find reserves of strength that will endure as long as life lasts. – RACHEL CARSON

Yesterday I had the privilege of attending the final hour or so of our church's Earth Camp at our retreat center, Koinonia, near Annandale. I arrived around lunch time to find a group of campers headed back from the dining room to their cabin. Instead of walking along the paved path, they headed directly into the woods. When one young girl saw me walking from my car, she threw up her hands and waved. "It's me! Emma!" I see her nearly every Sunday. And yet she must have thought that, here in the woods, I would not recognize her. I greeted her and the other campers and watched as they turned and walked into the grove of trees, their feet making a silent path on dirt, stone, and dead leaves. Over the last few days, they had become children of the woods.

A little later, as we gathered for a closing worship time, I asked the campers to tell me what they had experienced, what they had learned, what new thing had come to them over their days at Earth Camp. I heard tales of fishing, boating, swimming. I heard about how they had learned about recycling, how to use energy more responsibly, how to be more careful about their garbage. Others talked about how they had learned to walk more gently on the Earth. One girl said she had been frightened of the daddy-long-legs that had been near her bed but then learned that they ate the mosquitoes. She swore they had saved her from being bitten!

When I watched their young faces light up with the stories of new friends and all the fun they had experienced, I felt so grateful that these young ones had been given the gift of being in the woods. Richard Louv, author of *Last Child in the Woods*, writes about saving our children from nature-deficit disorder. He speaks of all the children who never have the chance to walk aimlessly on wooded paths, observe birds and other small animals in their natural habitat, experience their human

connection with a daddy-long-legs. He says: "The child in nature is an endangered species, and the health of children and the health of the Earth are inseparable."

As I helped these children load their now dirty belongings into the vans that will take them back to well-manicured lawns and city and suburban neighborhoods, I felt a sense of hope. Hope for the children and for the Earth. While not all children will have the experience of watching the small toads hop from shore to water home or see the great blue heron land its enormous body on a nest just feet away from where they are swimming, these twenty-seven children had. Their band-aided knees and bug-bit arms and legs showed the signs of an encounter with nature. And it was good—very, very good. Perhaps they will tell their friends and next year a whole new crop of children will head to the woods to learn, to have fun, to be changed. The connections will be made again and reinforced that we humans are guests on this precious planet. We share our present and our future with creatures with many legs, enormous wings, and fragile lives.

And we are all in it together.

Practice

Do you know a child who could use an outdoor adventure? Is that child you? Spend time outside today, no matter the weather, and look with a child's eyes at the world around.

Staring

A lake is the landscape's most beautiful and expressive feature. It is Earth's eye; looking into which the beholder measures the depth of his own nature.
– HENRY DAVID THOREAU, *Walden*

There are many things that I believe I can claim to be true. One of them is that the ability to stare at nearly any body of water can, for the most part, cure what ails a person. I have pulled myself up at the shore of these curing waters over the last two days. Visiting a friend's cabin, I have spent much of my time either sitting on the dock or on the overstuffed couch inside the cabin staring through the window at the glassiness of Little Boy Lake. The first few minutes of staring is often just spent taking in the lay of the lake—cabins to the right, YMCA camp to the left, sailboats anchored like birthday candles on the surface of the water, trees in various shades of green in their full summer glory, a few fishing boats here and there. It can often take an hour or more for the monkey mind of my daily life to switch off, until I can allow the vision of the lake in its stillness to begin to seep into me.

Eventually, if I can allow myself to be present to the water long enough, I can begin that slow movement into breathing with the lake. Watching the wind make its shifts on the water, I can feel my own breathing slowing, changing, as I perhaps remember that water world in which I, in which we all, had our beginning.

With more than 10,000 lakes dotting the Minnesota landscape, one of the gifts of summer is that, with little effort, we have the opportunity for "lake staring" within reach. Even city dwellers need only go a few miles before arriving at water's edge. There is something about being present to the water, about allowing the shape and condition of the lake to wash over the state of being human, that is transformative. When I think of the many healing stories of Jesus, I am reminded that so many of

them happened by the lakeside. While the disciples may have found themselves in desperate straights, riding out storms or eating on the beach, they seemed to always be changed by the encounter of Jesus on or near the water. Perhaps the scripture writers left out the parts where staring was involved!

Last night we sat and observed four loons who seemed simply to be riding on the water. Their rhythm of bobbing and diving became a focal point. As the day was drawing to a close, their black shiny bodies and white accents of feathers shone against the glistening water. Their red eyes were attentive to the human ones who were sharing their environment. They were, no doubt, skeptical. Every now and then one would lift its body slightly off its water bed and flap its wings as if to resettle into a more comfortable position. I found myself breathing with their floating and gasping at their water dance. What does it mean to share space with such a gorgeous creature? It seemed such a blessing.

After two-and-a-half days I will return to the regular rhythm of my daily life, to the lists of what needs to be accomplished, to meetings and laundry and all the tasks of being human, of living my life. If I am lucky, some place deep inside I will be able to recall the gentle lapping of the lake, how the time spent staring helped to heal my soul. If I have stared well, I might even be able to breathe the rhythm of the lake once again.

Practice

Try to spend some time near water today. Or if this is not possible, search through magazines until you find a picture of a lake or ocean. Use your imagination to breathe with the water until your mind calms and your soul rests.

Goals of Summer

Summer is the time when one sheds one's tensions with one's clothes, and the right kind of day is jeweled balm for the battered spirit. A few of those days and you can become drunk with the belief that all's right with the world. – ADA LOUISE HUXTABLE

This morning as I walked out the door I detected the faint scent of fall in the air. I shook the thought and smell out of my head. It is too soon to be turning the corner toward autumn. There are still too many things to do to savor the gifts of summer. I have not picked raspberries yet, or blueberries. I have not seen the North Shore in its summer finery. I have not had nearly enough ice cream cones or watermelon or red, juicy tomatoes. There is still too much to squeeze out of these precious days.

Summer is a time of opportunity. A time to try new things, master a new skill. Like the person inside a house I walked by on my walk today. The sounds of novice drumming filled the air. Bang! Crash! Ta-dum-ta-dum! All in broken, tentative rhythm. For this person it must be the "summer of learning to play the drums." I was reminded of the different summer goals I've set for myself over the years: learn to sew, do a swan dive, drive a car, read all the Nancy Drew mysteries, twirl a fire baton, learn the hula-hoop. Hour after warm hour, I remember working to perfect these new skills that require the leisurely time only summer can provide. Do you remember similar things from your own childhood or adolescence?

Further along on my walk, I was greeted by a cheery "Hi!" Two fresh-faced four-year-old girls were lining up a croquet set and a bag of tennis balls at the edge of the front porch. "Guess what?" the one with Pippi Longstocking braids asked. "We get to have a picnic tonight. We get to decorate the table and we are planning all the games." I had never seen these two girls before in my life, and yet they talked animatedly about the summer fun they were preparing. One girl had some red, blue, and yellow face

paint that had now merged with her sweaty, little skin, giving her face the appearance of a melting rainbow. They beamed their excitement and anticipation of the night's festivities toward me. For them, it could be their "summer of planning parties."

Today marks nearly the middle of July, a midsummer marker of sorts. There is still time to set a summer goal. What might you use these warm and long days to accomplish? Is it time to dust off the piano keys or pick up the guitar again? Has your bicycle been out of the garage yet? Have you always wanted to enter something in the state fair? (There's still time!) Or what about that monstrous novel you've been wanting to read (or write) forever?

There's no time like the middle of July to grab summer by the horns and fulfill a long-held dream. Come September the drummer down the street may be in a band. What goal would you like to accomplish in what's left of summer?

Practice

No matter the season, is there something you've been longing to do for which you never find the time? Why not today?

Savoring the Threshold

These are the days to savor. These final days of summer conjure up such joy, such gratitude, such beauty, that it seems to me the only logical response is to drink them in . . . slowly. As I write this, a gentle breeze is blowing outside and is floating in through our open windows. The air conditioning that kept us sane and comfortable last week has been turned off, silenced. Who knows if we will need the gift of it again? We found this morning that the sun was showing every streak and blotch on the windows. So, like in spring when the sunshine flows in and shows winter's dirt and grime, the windows of summer begged to be washed of their heated-filled, dusty film.

These days are threshold times. The days still hold enough warmth to require short sleeves by midday, but the morning requires a jacket and long pants. Soon the light-weight clothes will be packed away, and we Minnesotans will begin our layering fashion parade. But for now there is the act of savoring. Savoring the sunshine, the green yards and trees, the chill of the air and its cousin, heat. Gardens are beginning to bring out purples and lavenders attracting butterflies, a sea of flying color. On this threshold between what was and what is yet to be, we stand with our arms held out to receive.

Earlier this week I saw the first v-formation of geese who were perhaps practicing their eventual exit. It was a poignant sight. I thought of all this summer has held. While I will not fly off like the geese, there will be things that must be left behind. Things from which I, too, must fly. Such is the case with all the seasons of our lives. Though the life of this summer has shone with color and beauty, growth, and new life, even these things will eventually become brown, dry, fodder for a period of rest, reflection, death, and hope-filled renewal.

What are you savoring in these waning days of summer? What gifts of these last months have brought new life? What might the winds of autumn have in store? It seems to me the work of paying attention to the seasons, which are pure gift, allows us to be in tune with the rhythms of the universe, the heartbeat of all Creation. Attention to these rhythms also reminds us that we are a part of something immense and something created by a loving hand, something that is, after all, a brilliant Mystery.

This morning I read these words by Caitlin Matthews:

> *I kindle my soul from the Autumn's sunlight, glow of life, glow of light, glow of love, be upon my being, my heart, my soul this Autumn day, from break of light till fall of night.*

This morning prayer is an encouragement to savor. I offer it to you in hopes that day's end will find you basking in the riches, and richness, of this day.

Practice

What is calling out to you to savor its presence in your life? Spend time with it. Honor it as the gift it is. Whatever begs to be savored may not last forever.

Hooked

The wisdom of the humble lifts their heads high, and seats them among the great. The bee is small among flying creatures, but what it produces is the best of sweet things. — SIRACH 11:1,3

Yesterday I heard a wonderful report on Minnesota Public Radio about a Minnesota woman who received a "genius" grant from the MacArthur foundation. This grant carries a gift of $500,000 for the recipients to continue the study in which they have been engaged. The recipient, Marla Spivak, has spent years studying the honeybee. In the report she was asked how she came to such work. She declared that she had been "hooked on bees" since she was eighteen years old. I laughed out loud in my car. Hooked on bees! I think of what it must have been like to discover your passion so early and to have continued its love throughout your life. And then to have received a coveted award for that same love.

Now, to most people, honeybees may not seem like very important beings. Certainly not worth such a grand prize. But Marla Spivak points out that honeybees pollinate a third of the food supply of fruits and vegetables in the United States. Without their work, our lives will become less healthy. Something to think about, isn't it? Those little insects that buzz around the flowers and sweet drinks we hold on our decks on sunny days are important to our over-all well-being. And the truth is, they are not doing well. It seems that with diseases and pesticides and (can you believe this?) less flowers in the world, the honeybees are declining in numbers and in their own ability to do their work. And so the point needs to be made: If the honeybees aren't doing well, what about we two-leggeds who can sometimes walk about as if we are the center of the universe?

This all made me think about what other beings in our world we might be ignoring or overlooking simply because they seem smaller and, to us, insignificant. I happen

to be one of those people that believes that each part of Creation has a purpose. Sometimes, in my limited life experience, in my narrow understanding, I don't always honor this truth. But hearing about the honeybees yesterday gave me a reason to keep my eyes open, to be on alert, lest I think myself more important than I am. It was a good wake-up call.

There is a story I have heard more than once about the ways in which the rabbis used to help their students understand the sweetness of the scriptures. They would fill a tray with a thin layer of honey. Then they would have the students write the Hebrew letters in the honey. After the letters had been formed, the students would be instructed to lick the honey off their fingertips. As the sweetness slid off their fingers, onto their tongues and down their throats, the gift of the scriptures literally became a part of the aspiring writers. It is a wonderful image isn't it?

Perhaps those of us who travel life's sweet path today might take a moment to be present to all the small creatures with whom we travel. We might pause and think about what they bring to our lives and how we would be less without them. And then we might say a prayer of gratitude for the ants and worms that plow our garden dirt and the box elder bugs covering our window screens. For the squirrels busily gathering food for their winter sleep. For the bats which swoop and the mosquitoes that fly. And especially for the honeybee on which we depend. Even when we don't know it.

And while we are at it, how about a prayer for the ones who get hooked on these creatures and can bring us to a greater appreciation.

Practice

Notice the small ones today. Notice all that is smaller than you are. Notice and learn from them all the lessons they have to teach. And give thanks.

In the Flow

What makes a river so restful to people is that it doesn't have any doubt—it is sure to get where it is going and it doesn't want to go anywhere else. – HAL BOYLE

Yesterday was an absolutely stupendous day. The fall colors are beginning to emerge. The sun was shining so brightly, sending shafts of light through the yellows and reds that are beginning to paint the trees in our landscape. Even at the height of the day, there was just a hint of chill in the air. Children in our neighborhood were running around, playing, yelping, as if trying to squeeze the last bit of freedom out of the days they had known in summer. It was one of those days when a t-shirt was not enough. A jacket was too much. Some might even be so bold as to call it a "heavenly day."

We took the opportunity to wind our way down the river, taking in the half-harvested fields of corn and summer's exit. Brilliant green shown on one farm while others were dotted with the nubs of corn mowed to the edge of the ground. Flocks of birds could be seen overhead doing their little lacey dances in air. I love this autumn flight show they do. I always try to turn on the radio so the music can accompany their flights of fancy. No matter the tune on the dial, the music seems to fit. They, like the children, seemed to be making a last ditch effort at soaking up the sunshine, the warmth, the gifts of frivolous days gone by.

At the edge of the Mississippi River, we sat watching the powerful waters make their turns in some of the widest areas of the river's path. The waters seemed even more treacherous than usual, fueled by the heavy rains we experienced last week. We sat and watched as enormous, rootless, trees floated alongside smaller branches and limbs torn loose by strong winds and the rains that are playing even greater havoc further down river. Floating along in the current was also debris of all sorts: plastic soda bottles, all kinds of aluminum cans, papers, plastic, an upended paper plate (how did it stay afloat?). A Styrofoam cup half filled with

muddy water stood upright as if someone might reach out, pick it up, and take a drink. And the most unusual: a black and white Adidas sport sandal riding the water as if making a miraculous, one-legged walk on the waves. The sight was both astounding and quite sad. This mighty river filled with such filth and pollution. My husband pointed out that, if all went well for some of the debris, it would be in New Orleans in a couple of days. A tragic but interesting thought.

Later we walked another path further north along the river. A plaque along the way pointed out that people had walked, lived, and flourished along this river for 8,000 years. An amazing idea! As I looked out toward the burgeoning waters flowing around islands of trees and docks that seemed to be free floating, I wondered about those people. What manner of things had my genetic ancestors seen float by 8,000 years ago? 5,000 years ago? 1,000 years ago? 100 years ago? Surely the floods, which are predictable and a part of how Creation works, have always caused debris to make its way from our end of the river to the gulf that will receive it. How has that changed over the years? What does the "stuff" we send down the river have to say about who we are now?

I don't have any answers to these questions. But I did leave that experience feeling a greater connection to those ancient people who made their lives, their homes by the shores of the river. I felt a connection and an obligation to walk gently on this land. Perhaps some day, say 1,000 years from now, someone will stand at the river's edge and wonder about me and my life companions. Perhaps they will wonder if we loved the river, if we felt its connection to our living and to our brothers and sisters who share its flow. I pray they will think on us kindly.

Practice

Spending time by a body of water can be good for the soul. If possible, spend some time near a lake, a river, an ocean, and imagine what needs to be washed away in your life, falling gently into the moving water. If this is impossible, try the same act with the water in your kitchen sink.

Way

As you start on the Way, the Way appears. – RUMI

These past days, with the rain coming down and the darker days descending as autumn approaches, have been good for self-reflection. It seems, for me, that fall always conjures up this inner work. Maybe it is just the school year rhythm that is so firmly planted within us that gets this movement happening. But whatever it is, I welcome it. And this fall I am particularly aware of it given an upcoming pilgrimage to Scotland. Those of us who are embarking on this adventure continue to affirm that this is not merely a trip but a longing for transformation.

Of course, one need not be heading off to far away places to be attentive to the unfolding of our life's path. This is a gift that is present to us with the rising of each new day, at the beginning of each season, each year. The Quakers often speak of this presence to our unfolding life simply as "Way." Most often, however, our human inclination is to stumble after things we think are outside of us, outside our reach. These are goals after which we strive. And yet, over the years I have come to believe that everything we need to do the work to which we are called, to be our authentic self, our God-created self, is present within us from the beginning. This discovering and uncovering of the way in which we are to walk is a life-long process. Our circumstances, often created by others, can bump up against what we know to be true. The choices we make about those circumstances either help or hinder our discovery, our attention to Way. Does this ring true for you?

In the lives of the early Christians, they often referred to Jesus' teaching, even Jesus himself, as the Way. I love this idea. It helps move people away from the traditional practice of speaking about belief and places the emphasis on how, as people of faith, we pay attention to Jesus' living, how he moved in the world, walked his path, created his Way of being in relationship with the Holy. This was what, I think, his life offers ours. Belief keeps us in our heads and often has been

designed to keep others out of the circle while declaring how right the "believers" are. Attending to walking the Way of Jesus, while perhaps more challenging, opens our hearts, softens our hearts to one another, to the world.

Sometimes the Way, as the Quakers put it, is a path that is full of shadows, maybe even completely dark. These become difficult times for the one who is walking the path and often for those who stand by the side of the road with only their love as an offering. And yet I am somehow comforted and inspired by the words of Medieval mystic Meister Eckhart who describes this challenging life time as "the Wayless Way, where the Sons [and Daughters] of God lose themselves and, at the same, find themselves."

Isn't this almost always how it goes? We awake each day with a notion of what the day (or our life) may hold, what we have planned for it to become. We walk out into the world and sometimes our plans work out just as we hoped. But often Way calls to us from someplace just outside our vision, tugging at something that is planted deep within. We can choose to be open or not, to follow or run away. We can choose to change our route, make a course correction, close our eyes and hide. Though it may not always seem as if the choice is ours, it really is. If we have the courage and the heart to listen to the Spirit's movement, Way will open.

No way, you say? Way!

Practice

Spend time reflecting on the path of your life. Where has Way opened for you? What doors have closed? How has this closing also been an opening to a new Way?

Time Travel

The last several days have been a whirlwind. Friday morning I headed out to Seattle to accompany our youngest son back to his second year of college. This falls in the realm of: Where did the time go? It was a short trip of two days. Factoring in the time change, it has made for a fuzzy sense of time. What day is it? Why am I sleepy right now? Questions like these are dancing around the frontal lobe.

Today as I moved from meeting to meeting, I have recognized the privilege with which I was able to do such a thing. Beyond the privilege, there is also the speed, the sense of entering another part of the country and the gift of noticing how what seems novel and interesting to me about life in another place is something those who witness it daily might find mundane. I, for one, could not imagine taking for granted the daily passage of ferries, much less the beauty of Puget Sound. I cannot imagine coming to see the color and eccentricities of Pike Place Market as anything short of astounding.

And yet there are probably people who walk past these sights daily and do not notice. There are probably those who rush from work to home, from school to their car, without thinking twice about the beauty and wonder that is theirs to behold. What we have on our plate, in our sight, often is overlooked in our everyday rounds. We simply don't have the presence of mind to see.

That is why my experience on the flight out was so memorable. As we were approaching the Seattle airport, the pilot said over the sound system that if we looked out the windows to our left, we would be able to see Mt. Rainier. If we looked out the right side of the plane, we would be able to see both Mt. Hood and Mt. Baker.

Sure enough! There they were. Above the clouds that settled over the ground below, the sun was shining boldly on these signature mountains.

But the best part was watching the people strain their necks to see these massive, snow-covered peaks. My seat partner, a stranger to me, leaned back and pointed out the window, letting me in on the sight, sharing the gift of this moment with me. I looked around as others on the plane made similar gestures. Smiles were all around as we shared in this mid-air glimpse of majesty and wonder.

I hope I always have the presence of mind to see the things in my own daily life with the fresh eyes of a visitor, even a tourist. I hope I see, open my arms, and point—all the time wearing a big smile.

Practice

What sights in your daily round have you stopped seeing? Tuck a small piece of paper in your pocket and jot down the many amazing things you see today. Before you sleep tonight, offer a prayer for the wonder of your life.

Tree Memory

I have this belief, a deeply held belief, that we human beings travel much of our lives in search of understanding who we really are, why we are here, where we have been, and how we are to live in the world in our time and place. In that searching we also carry within us the gifts of our ancestors we know and those that are mystery to us. Of course, most of us do not think of this minute to minute, even hourly or daily. But, every now and then, we have a moment where we glimpse something that lies deep within us. We don't always understand why our eyes tear up at some experience or at overhearing a phrase. We don't quite fathom why this particular sunset seems richer than others or this view of a lake tugs at our hearts. We don't always understand how a place we've never been before feels so familiar. All we know is that when these experiences happen, they are profound. Often fleeting, but still profound.

This morning I had one of those experiences. I sat and had coffee at a park near our home. I have walked by this park hundreds of times, have taken my children to play on the playground there. But today I became completely aware of the grove of trees that make up this park. I vividly saw their shapes and their spacing, how they formed a canopy of shade and protection for those animals and people who walk through and play in this park. I was aware of their aliveness and how my aliveness was somehow connected to theirs. I furrowed my brow but held on to the feeling.

Later, I drove down Summit Avenue in St. Paul. I do this periodically, taking in the beautiful houses, the regal lawns, the exquisite landscaping. It makes the regular drive to work more a trip to the art museum rather than the daily schlog. Again, I became aware of how, down the boulevard, the trees are planted in a canopy that creates a pathway of green. Down this pathway, through these trees, humans walked and ran. I take this same drive nearly every Sunday morning and yet I had never seen that particular protective formation of the trees before. Another brow

furrowing. And yet both these experiences of trees connected with me at some deep level, a depth I could not quite put my finger on.

And then I remembered a bit of what I was reading last night before I went to sleep. I have been reading *The Mist-Filled Path: Celtic Wisdom for Exiles, Wanderers and Seekers* by *Frank MacEowen in preparation for my upcoming pilgrimage to Scotland. MacEowen writes:

> *We Celts are lovers of trees. On one day in particular when I was out in the trees, something happened. I had a sudden and shocking remembrance of the trees as guardians, allies, and as conduits for activating memory. . . . In that moment the trees suddenly told me that they were my ancient home, that I had known them intimately before, and that one day I would live among them again.*

Perhaps the reading of this book influenced my experience this morning. Or maybe I was simply more awake and open to the world this day. Who knows? But I guess that each of us has certain ancestral memories that are planted deep in our cells, deep in our minds and hearts. These memories can be awakened at the oddest, yet perfect, moments.

This morning my Celtic ancestors paid a visit.

Practice

Stand firmly with your feet planted a few inches apart. Feel your feet on the ground and connect with the bottoms of your feet. Imagine them growing roots that move down into the earth. Reach your arms above your head, toward the sky. Imagine them reaching into the heavens. Feel your body, like a tree trunk connecting you to earth and to heaven. Breathe deeply and know the presence of the Holy connecting you to all this is.

Turning the Page

Education is not filling a pail but the lighting of a fire. – WILLIAM BUTLER YEATS

Today marks a turning of the page. Whether or not there are children returning to school in your household, or if you are returning to school yourself, today marks the beginning of fall and all the season brings with it. Last night the winds seemed to pick up with a felt ferocity that blew away all summer had held. Winds were so strong I began to imagine them cleaning the slate for a fresh start. And don't we all need this every now and then? Today children will find themselves caught up in a routine that looks nothing like their summer life. Some will embrace this. Others will not. But all will be changed by the turning of this page.

Autumn brings with it shorter days and colder temperatures. This requires an attention to what we wear and how we plan our days. No more grabbing a t-shirt and shorts, ones that may have been on the floor from yesterday's wear. Instead, there must be an attention to layers and the fickle temperatures of these changing days. Some are as warm as summer only to turn bitterly cold by day's end. As we layer on clothing, we also take on new ideas, new experiences, and wear them like jackets that bring us warmth or comfort.

But it is the rhythm of the change of seasons that calls to me. As I watched the children this morning waiting for their buses, I thought of what lies ahead for them in this change. New things will be learned, challenges will be overcome, successes and mistakes will be made. There will be new friends and mentors they never expected. I have already heard children I know look forward to the milestones they will experience this year: being in the class that goes to the state capitol, getting their Bible as a third-grader, beginning in confirmation, graduating from high school, going off to college. So many pages, large and small, that turn in our lives.

As we grow older, if we allow ourselves, we can see this time of year as a time to turn a page also. The wind that blew throughout the night and threatened (or promised) to continue today offers itself as a slate-cleaner. What pages are ready to turn for you? What adventurous experience do you want to embrace? What new friend do you want to make? How do you need to be mentored?

The pages of summer have come to an end. But the story of autumn is yet to written. How we choose to embrace the ever-turning pages of our lives is a gift, a gift not to be taken lightly. Come winter—and make no mistake it will arrive—what will you have learned? How will you spend these glorious days of autumn?

As the page turns, let the new story begin.

Practice

What goal or hope do you have for the next season. Write it down. Place it someplace where you will see it and recommit to it every day. Tell a least one person about this hope and ask them to check in with you about it. Give yourself to it every day until it becomes a hope fulfilled.

In the Company of Sheep

During our recent travels in Scotland, the one constant besides the enormous breakfasts was the presence of sheep. At first glance there is the "cute" factor that these wooly beings conjure. But as I spent more and more time observing them, walking quite near them, and being present to them, I realized these four-leggeds have much to teach us. Here are just some of the gleanings of being in the company of sheep:

First, sheep are fully present to the moment. Whether in a flat, lushly green pasture or at the top of a craggy moor, sheep are present to their environment. Humans may rush by. Jets may roar overhead. Other animals may encroach on their space. They continue to be calm and at home wherever their journey of the day has taken them.

Sheep are flexible. They seem to be as happy grazing in a pasture as they are at the top of a mountain. Winds may whip up around them; they are not fazed. Rain may pour down, creating mud and muck; they never vary their pace. The sun may come out, a rainbow may shine over their heads; they remain grounded, standing in beauty. They take the ebb and flow of life's challenges in stride.

Several times I had the opportunity to be up close and personal with sheep. Here is what I noticed: Sheep, like dogs, seem to be an animal that actually will look you in the eye. In approaching one or two sheep, I was unsure of what my move should be, what theirs might be. And so I simply looked into their oddly pupiled eyes. We seemed to come to some understanding that "all shall be well" and that co-existing, four-legged and two-legged was an OK thing.

And speaking of co-existing, perhaps the most amazing thing I observed was how sheep don't need to be surrounded by their own kind to be happy, to be content. One afternoon on the island of Iona, I was hiking out to the North Beach. I watched as a sheep was lying meditatively in the pasture. As he lie there, a crow

landed on his head. The sheep did not budge. I could not believe my eyes. But then, it got even better. That crow lifted into the air, and a different crow landed on the sheep's head while the first crow made a perch on the sheep's back. And then, if only to confound me more, the second crow flew up, joined the first crow on the sheep's back, and a third crow landed on the head of the sheep. Still, the sheep sat calmly co-existing with his feathered companions. A trinity of birds on the body of the sheep. This may sound unbelievable, but I have witnesses.

And so, after all these encounters in the company of sheep, it became even clearer to me the depth of the lessons of Jesus that centered around these humble animals. As a person who was also often surrounded by sheep, he, too, must have seen the wisdom of their daily walk. As he wove stories to teach us of the kingdom of God, why wouldn't the sheep show up in the telling? After all, they know how to be present to the movement of the Spirit. They are flexible and find ways to graze wherever they can. They are calm, grounded witnesses to the world around them. They look you in the eye, acknowledging your presence. And they live and play well with others. Certainly all these traits are ones humans could emulate.

In Luke, Jesus tells the story of the shepherd who has a hundred sheep. At the end of the day, in his accounting of his flock, he only finds ninety-nine and proceeds to go on a search to find the lost sheep. "Which one of you, having a hundred sheep and losing one of them, does not leave the ninety-nine in the wilderness and go after the one that is lost until he finds it?" asks Jesus.

I wonder if the lost one was the sheep who would let three crows rest on it?

Practice

Follow the example of sheep today. Be present in the moment. Be flexible. Co-exist with all Creation's beings, even the human ones. Look others in the eye. Play well with all you meet. Be a witness.

Beginning

Sometimes we have difficulty believing we will see anything new. After all, we know the story. We've heard it year after year. What could we possibly see or hear that we have not seen or heard before?

– MARY LOU REDDING, *While We Wait: Living the Questions of Advent*

Advent . . . the beginning. Yesterday was the beginning of the new church year, the first Sunday in Advent. Christian churches everywhere began their walk into a new year. During this short season that leads us toward the celebration of Christmas, we use words like "anticipation," "expectation," "waiting," "watching," to describe the spirit of these days. We watch and wait for the birth of the Christ in our midst. We anticipate a time when God's presence among us will be visible, palpable, a time when the human family will live in the full light of the Holy. Like the gospel writers who committed this story to print, we each have our own unique ways of how we believe this manifestation will come to be.

As I look out my office window right now, the skies are gray, and snow and rain are spitting against the glass. The large oak tree which keeps me company daily, its strong presence a constant source of inspiration, is dripping in the starkness of the day. Advent comes to those of us in this part of the country during the darkest, often most somber part of the year. And yet this season holds within it the warmth and light of all that can be born from just such bleakness. Candles will be lit. Food will be shared. Gifts will be given. Hopes will be shared. Stories will light up the eyes of children, the heart of memory will beat for those who are older. Sacred texts will tell of a surprising God who shows up in the most unexpected places.

Our work during this time is to follow the command of Matthew: "Keep awake, for you do not know on what day your God is coming." Our work becomes the practice of being present for all the ways in which the Holy comes to us, not only in December,

but each day. Even in the madness that can become what we call Christmas, our work is to be always watchful for the goodness, the love, the kindness, the joy, that creeps into the most mundane and marvelous experiences that come our way. How will we see God . . . even in places we don't want to believe possible? Like the mall. Or traffic. Or Christmas music that is played over and over again. Or the newscast that tells of war in far-off lands. Or the young man who holds the sign at the corner stoplight. Or the politician whose ideas drive us to distraction.

For in truth, God's presence moves through all this and more. As people who watch and wait for the coming of Christ, how can we open our hearts to welcome the Child that lives in each of those we meet, in all the places where Breath moves? How can we make time and space for welcoming the Christ child that waits to be born to us?

Advent . . . beginning. What is beginning in you on this bleak, dark day?

Practice

Find a signal that will remind you to "keep awake." Perhaps it is the ring of your phone, the red of a stoplight, the beginning of each hour. Spend a few moments being awake to your breath, your presence in this perfect moment.

Hidden Joys

I have a friend who is so deeply connected with God that he can see joy where I expect only sadness. He travels much and meets countless people. When he shares, he tells of the hidden joys he has found: someone who brought him hope and peace . . . little groups of people who are faithful to each other in the midst of turmoil . . . the small wonders of God. And I am disappointed sometimes because I want to hear "newspaper news," exciting and exhilarating stories. But he never responds to my need for sensationalism. He just says, "I saw something very small and very beautiful, something that gave me much joy."

– HENRI NOUWEN, *Return of the Prodigal Son*

In Days to Come . . . Great Joy. This is our church's theme for Advent. Once again I am coming face to face with the concept that, once you begin to live into one of these themes, once you start thinking about a particular word or phrase, similar words begin to pop up everywhere. It happened to me this morning when I opened a newsletter I receive monthly. This quote by the beloved priest Henri Nouwen was tucked in at the bottom of one of the pages. I shook my head and thought: "Here we go. Joy will be cropping up everywhere." There certainly could be worse things, right?

Joy. What does this word mean to you? Is joy the same thing as happiness? How does one achieve joy? Or is there even really anything we can *do* to claim this rich three-lettered prize? I had this conversation with two friends yesterday. As we walked further and further into joy-talk, we probably had more questions than answers. We agreed that being "in pursuit" of joy rarely works. It usually leads mostly to disappointment, a loss of something that never existed based on expectations that were created out of a deep longing. I think we agreed that joy comes to us . . . most often in the smallest events and through something over which we have very little control. But when joy makes its entrance, we know it.

On Sunday, I offered people small booklets that simply had the words "Great Joy" on the cover. I invited people to make a note about the experiences in their day that had brought them joy, perhaps even great joy. I suggested that this could become a practice during Advent. To be present to the joy that comes our way every day—not just on the mountain top days like Christmas or our birthday— but every day. Writing down these moments of joy, I believe, could provide us with the opportunity to see where joy brushes past us, bringing a blessing to the ordinary movements of our life. The journal of these blessings could also provide an opportunity to honor those moments and offer our gratitude to a Universe that longs to have delight in us.

Where have you experienced joy already in this day? This day which is a gift, never to be repeated? Perhaps if we are awake and aware of the joy that is already present in our own lives we might have the courage—and it does take courage—to reach out and offer a joy-filled act to another. I am imagining a pyramid scheme that is actually a good thing, that actually brings benefit to all involved. Joy building on joy.

Sounds to me like a pretty good way to walk the days of Advent.

Practice

OK. Begin to take stock of the things that bring you joy. Write them down. Tell someone about them. Offer your thanks.

Just in Time

> *An artist is merely someone with good listening skills who accesses the creative energy of the Universe to bring forth something on the material plane that wasn't there before. It was a part of Spirit before we could see it as a book, a painting, a ballet, a film.* – SARAH BAN BREATHNACH

Over the weekend, we received the first snow fall of the season. And I have to go on record and say it was just in time! I had mentioned to a friend earlier in the week that the continuing good weather had begun to wear on me and mess with my internal, creative rhythms. You see, I need a certain amount of incubation time that only winter seems to provide. For me, there is nothing like the ruminating that can happen when snow has rendered travel a less than viable option. There is nothing like staring out the window as the flakes fall slowly to the ground, transforming the landscape before your very eyes, knowing that the only wise track to take is to stay put. Oh, rain will do in a creative pinch, and it provides its own inspiration, but a snowfall holds within it danger, romance, frivolity, and sheer magic. What better way to feed your inner muse than by being gripped by a snowstorm? No matter your creative outlet—cooking, knitting, painting, writing, napping—a good snowstorm will never disappoint.

This year, the way in which the summer/autumn seemed to want to be the guest that wouldn't leave, was stalling my winter mulling. Internally, you see, I sense Advent's imminent arrival and have a desire to ruminate on the gifts of this mysterious, life-bearing season. But how to do that with the roses still blooming on the stems outside the church? It seemed impossible to me to think of planning for all December offers while some people were still walking around in shorts!

Quote by Sarah Ban Breathnach from Simple Abundance: A Daybook of Comfort and Joy *by Sarah Ban Breathnach. Used by permission of Hachette Book Group.*

Now I know the seasons are not imperative for many people to get in touch with their creative side. After all, much creative work happens in warm months, and creativity flourishes in warm and wonderful places. But for those of us who need the incubation that going into the cave of darkness and cold provides, much like returning to the womb, there is nothing better than the experience of the first snowfall. "Now," we say, " the real work begins. Now the reflective life calls. Now is the time to stare into the middle distance while the poem takes form, while the problem is solved, while the seeds take root."

For those of you who find your muse of creativity in the warm, summer-like months, God bless you. Those of us who need the gifts that only ice, snow, and dark days can offer beg your indulgence. The fact is the world needs us all. The world needs the creativity of summer sun dancers and winter blues artists. The world needs the heat of a good steamy novel and the longing of a sparse poem. So let's celebrate the dance of the seasons and the different and unique blessings they bring. Whether sun or snow, brilliant light or brooding darkness, whether ice or flowering beauty, there is enough inspiration for everyone if we are awake to its presence.

And isn't that the most amazing thing of all? So, get cracking. Pull out those paint brushes and sharpen the pencils. Clear off the table and dig out the 2000-piece puzzle of Monet's "Waterlilies." Buy some yeast and bake a loaf of hearty bread. Write a letter to a dear friend who lives across the country. Sit down at the piano and play show tunes. Sing at the top of your lungs until the neighbors look out their windows.

Snow is on the ground. Let the creativity begin!

Practice

What creative project is nudging you? What act of creation is waiting to come to birth through your spirit, your hands, your heart? There could be no better day to begin than this day. This very day.

Kitchen Geologist

Our family has always been collectors of stones. While on vacations we come home with our pockets filled with stones from beaches, mountains, hiking paths, cabin yards. We carry them back wrapped in dirty socks, tucked into toiletry bags, inside shoes, and in leftover sandwich bags. We then often add them to our garden and the little fish pond in the backyard. But most of the many faceted stones we have collected as souvenirs of our travels end up in our home. They rest in bowls, often with water covering them, so they continue to give off the sheen that attracted our eyes to them in the first place.

I have just such a small bowl of stones in our kitchen right now. I have moved it from the counter to the center of the stove and back again. It began its journey in our home on the kitchen table. Any place where I can be sure my eyes will fall on the unusual green stones several times a day. These are stones I picked up in St. Columba's Bay on the Island of Iona. They range in shades from a deep, dark forest green to a nearly gaudy lime green. There are several that are speckled white and green, orangish-brown and green, like little birds' eggs. I chose them from the beach after a three-hour pilgrimage across farmland, a golf course, past a heather ringed mountain loch, and on rocky trails. Our guide told us that, if we were lucky, we might find a completely iridescent green stone known as St. Columba's Tears.

St. Columba reached the bay of this tiny Scottish island in 563 A.D. after fleeing from Ireland where he had been a priest, an artist, a poet, a prophet. He had copied and illuminated some of the scriptures and kept them for his own which caused, so the story goes, a battle to break out and many people were killed. He and his monks fled Ireland and landed on this tiny Scottish island only to turn back toward the sea and realize they could not see, nor return to, their beloved homeland. They say as he wept on the beach, for the lives lost and the land he

loved, his tears fell to the ground and the stones turned this brilliant green. It is a lovely, sad story and a wonderful explanation for these beautiful stones.

I am not a geologist. I do not know what causes certain stones to be the way they are, the color they are, the shape or texture they are. But I love to think about the tears that have been shed in the world—for lost loves, homes, lives, dreams—and the idea that those tears might turn into something beautiful. Like a green stone. As I look on these stones resting in their white bowl, I know they are covered with good old St. Paul tap water and not the salt-infused ocean. But they carry, at some level I also do not understand, a story of a place and a people that now has seeped into my story. The tears shed on that beach—and I have no doubt there have been many—cannot be washed off or dried up, and so they must become a part of the stone itself.

As I move around my kitchen, making a meal or a cup of tea, I find my eyes gazing on the green stones that have become a part of my daily walk. I think of all the tears that will be shed this day. At hospital bedsides. On battlefields. In classrooms. At desks. In shelters. On sidewalks. Under bridges. On playgrounds. So many tears.

May the One who watches over all broken places and people take these tears and create something beautiful.

Practice

Walk gently in the world today. People everywhere are shedding tears. Imagine a stone in your hand or pick one up from a path you travel. Hold the stone and offer prayers of mercy for all those shedding tears.

A Small Reminder

Creating God, your fingers trace the bold design of farthest space;
Let sun and moon and stars and light and what lies hidden praise your might.

Sustaining God, your hands uphold Earth's myst'ries known or yet untold;
Let waters fragile blend with air, enabling life, proclaim your care.

Redeeming God, your arms embrace all now despised for creed or race;
Let peace, descending like a dove, make known on earth your healing love.

Indwelling God, your gospel claims one family with a billion names;
Let ev'ry life be touched by grace until we praise you face to face.

– JEFFREY ROWTHORN

Every now and then, I believe, we need a reminder about the magnitude of which we are a part. A couple of Sundays ago, we sang this song set to a beautiful tune by Minnesota composer David Haas. The music is haunting and sticks with you. But as our gathered community lifted their voices, it was the words that got stuck in me. As we were singing, I glanced around at people's faces and recognized that many were having similar feelings to my own. When we were finished I said my usual lead-in line to our time of announcements: "There are many ways to be involved in the life and work of this community this week." But instead of going on to all the many wonderful classes and opportunities, I invited people to take this hymn home and put on their fridge or in a place where they would see the words often during the coming week. On the following Monday morning, I posted it on my office door so I could read it as I would come and go. Those who came to my door might also be drawn into its power as they knocked or waited.

It is so easy for me, and I don't think I am alone in this, to get bogged down in the mundane details of any day and to forget that I am a part of an ancient and

unfolding story. This story of the Universe, this telling of God's movement in the world, is one in which we each play a very small part . . . but an important one. Our work is to be awake enough to remember that we are important to its unfolding.

Last night as I stood bathed in the blue light of a full winter moon, I felt how small I was in comparison to "the bold design of farthest space." But I also understand my work as a human to be one who speaks praise, awe, amazement, to point out the beauty and wonder by which we are surrounded. I had already pointed the moon out to my husband and his sister. And earlier I had done a similar thing with some colleagues as we left an evening meeting. Finally, I sent a text message to our son in Seattle: "Have you seen the moon tonight?" As I made my way to bed, I took a final glance out the window and noticed how the world which had been so white all day was now a brilliant blue. It seemed a moment of pure gift.

These moments, when we allow ourselves to be bathed in the mystery of what it means to be alive in our time, in this world, are ones in which we can know in a deep way what it means to be connected to all other humans everywhere. Awe is an experience that is not bound by creed or race, education or economics or status. It is quite simply something that brings a certain peace that is difficult to find words to express. And so I trust that in city or village, on many continents around our world, people are lifting their eyes toward what amazes them, what shows them the presence of the Holy. They are turning their attention from the little details that can wait. They are having an experience of grace, a fullness of knowing that we are a part of something big, something mysterious, something to be held gently and with reverence . . . praising that which some of us call God, face to face.

Practice

What mystery fills you with awe? Find an image of the Milky Way. Notice where Earth is in the splash of light. Think of where you fit into that picture. Breathe deeply and say "Ahhhhhh. . . ."

Dancing Crows

I am not sure if I am the only one noticing this phenomenon. But on these particularly cold days, when the sky is brilliant blue and the sunshine is blinding in its reflection off the mounds of snow that make up our landscape, flocks of crows are dancing in the sky. They seem to fly in a plenty that is not visible in summer. I watched yesterday as they soared in a dance that seemed to be accompanied by the music on my radio. Up and over, around and down, they formed black lace patterns against a dying day on my way home from work. I watched the flock form an undulating motion as, every now and then, one bird would peel off to land for a rest on a light pole or rooftop.

Perhaps it fascinates me because their posture is so very different from our human ones. Bundled up in down and fleece, our shoulders touch our ears as our lumpy forms plod along. We can seem to dance a penguin dance as we move across the icy pavement. But we all know that this is not a true dance, only a movement that tries to create a safety net that might prevent any real breakage should we fall.

And so the dance of these black, soaring birds elicits some desire of freedom in me. In one poem, Mary Oliver writes of how the crows will remember that even in the deep of winter that summer will return, that corn will be theirs again. I love the idea that crows, like me, are remembering the beuty and bounty of another season.

Traveling last weekend through the farm country of Minnesota and Wisconsin, I allowed my eyes to take in all the white fields that in just a few months will be green and tall and waving in the warm breezes. I remembered last summer and the joy I found in driving through just such farmland, reveling in the beauty and bounty of miles and miles of the work of people I did not know but admired still.

In that remembering, my shoulders relaxed, and the distance between my shoulders and ears grew. I felt all the tense muscles, held just so out of protection, relax into

warmness. I do not have the ability to fly, to dance in beautiful patterns riding on the frigid winds, but, if the poet is correct about crows, we both have a similar sense of gratitude. For the miracle of a sun-cold day and the hope of the corn yet to be. And to the Spirit that moves in it all.

Practice

There will be unusual sights that come your way today. Make note of them. Live into them. Notice the presence of Spirit in them.

Winter Hope

Yesterday at worship, during the prayers of the people, someone offered a prayer of gratitude for the seven seed catalogues that had arrived in her mailbox this past week. One for each day of the week! In most places this might seem an odd expression of thankfulness, but given the fact that in Minnesota we have not seen the ground since early October, everyone knew exactly what she meant. The snow that came early and has continued every day, minus two, in January is beginning to play with our minds. Our household has not received any of the winter blessings in the form of colored pictures of beautiful flowers and regular and exotic vegetables yet. But yesterday's prayer planted a certain sense of expectation. Now I will be vigilant as I watch each day's mail arrive. The catalogues are, after all, a sign of winter hope.

Hope comes to us in many ways. When we encounter a newborn baby, most of us would describe that experience as one of hope. We might even say, "God has said 'yes' to the world again." The rising of the sun every morning is also a sign of hope. Like our ancient ancestors we often sense the new opportunities that arrive with the beginning of that first ray of new light after the darkness of the night. The beginning of a new year can often signal a sense of hope, the chance to begin again, to right some wrongs, to recommit ourselves to change. Many experiences of hope are a natural part of the rhythm of life. Like the wisdom of the writer of Ecclesiastes, we know that "to everything there is a season." This kind of hope is simply another thread in the pattern of fabric we know as life.

But there is also, I believe, a hope we need to create, we need to feed. This kind of hope is a choice. It may be something to which we must commit ourselves even when it is invisible to us. Like the promise of the seeds that can be ordered in the midst of winter, we embrace a hope of what is to come, yet to be dreamed. Those

of us who are parents or have been teachers know this kind of hope-as-choice quite well.

I was reminded of this very fact yesterday afternoon as I participated in the funeral of one of our dear saints of the church. This amazing woman had been a pillar of our church and a life-long teacher and missionary. She had taught and served children in the Minneapolis public schools and also in Africa. I have had the privilege of knowing her for more than twenty years. We once even slept on the floor of a New Orleans church fellowship hall where we accompanied youth on a mission trip. I remember her laughter and how she clearly and gently led our youth and those we met in an orphanage where we assembled new beds for the children. She was a no-nonsense person who was also full of love. Love for church, for children, and for God.

As many people spoke about the gifts this faithful woman had imparted to them, I was struck with what hope she had planted in the world. She boldly and with deep commitment worked with children who could have been lost in the shuffle of society. But her belief in each as a beloved child of God allowed her to continue to help them rise to their best selves. Hopefully, each of us have had at least one person in our life who bestowed just such hope in the container of who we are.

In addition to this lovely woman, I have had the blessing of knowing her grandson when he was just a little boy. I had observed over the years, the doses of hope she had poured into him. And so, to now see this handsome young man stand confidently in his grief and speak of his grandmother, of her love for him and her church, brought tears to my eyes. As a journalist, he chose his words wisely and with expertise, just as she would have liked. He spoke eloquently about her life story and the good with which she moved in his life. He was clear in outlining what was truly important to her. The hope which she had planted in him was now being passed on through his education, his devotion, his love, his work.

Sometimes the colorless season of winter is real. Other times there are just days or weeks or years that need a good infusion of hope. A hope we choose. For all those who have chosen to have hope in us, may we give thanks this day. And may we choose to pay forward the many hopes that have been sent our way.

Practice

Choose hope this day. What is the shape of your hope? What is its color? How does it move in you and the world around you? Hold onto this hope with all your might.

Daily Rhythms

This day and this night,
May I know, O God,
The deep peace of the running wave
The deep peace of the flowing air
The deep peace of the quiet earth
The deep peace of the shining stars
The deep peace of the Child of Peace.
– J. PHILIP NEWELL, *Celtic Prayers from Iona*

Over the weekend I had the privilege of being on the North Shore, about an hour north of Duluth. Driving there in an intense fog, we arrived long after dark, to spend a few days with friends at a family cabin. The fog was so thick as we drove the last several miles that we had no landmarks to give us our bearings. All we knew was that every now and then the fog would clear, and we would catch a glimpse of the cold, sparkling waters of Lake Superior out the passenger window. Just as suddenly as it had appeared, we would again be plunged into the enveloping fog, and the lake would be gone from our sight once again.

Being an early riser, even while on vacation, I was awake the next morning to see the sun come up over the Big Lake. What had been invisible to me in the foggy night was now shining in the morning sun. As I sat watching the morning sky turn numerous shades of pastels—pale yellow, blue, turquoise, lavender—I was reminded of the many times the fog of night has obscured my ability to see what becomes clear by morning's light. I thought of the many times I have wrestled the fears and demons of the nighttime only to find myself calmer and better sighted in the pure light of morning. Perhaps you have had similar experiences.

From my picture window lookout I could see how the ice cold waters of winter had made coats for the enormous rocks that formed the cove in front of me. Large stone walls had been splashed by what had to have been tremendous waves, over and over again, until they now wore icy, thick layers forming what looked like icebergs. The waves were much calmer now, but I could still see the waves pushed and pulled by the strong winds. Dancing back and forth across the water, wind became visible.

That evening we were graced by the full moon making its presence known in the winter sky. Slowly it moved across the sky until it stood just in line with the cove, with the cabin's windows. A brilliant shaft of white light traveled from moon to the ice formations below. As we gazed at the moon bathing the earth in light, I thought of all the stories I have heard of children who beg their parents to give them the moon. This is not metaphor but real. They want that big, shiny, round jewel. At that moment, it would have seemed to me like the most natural thing to want to reach up and take possession of the moon. Such beauty!

To be present to the daily rhythms of sunrise and sunset is a gift and something we rarely, in our fast paced world, allow ourselves to notice. Of course, sunrise and sunset over Lake Superior gives this practice a certain profound nature. But, I wonder, how might my life be different if, for just one week, I would be present, really present to both the rising and the setting of the sun. How would it help put everything else that happens in a day in perspective? Somehow I think it might be something to consider. Do you?

I think of the ancient Celts who had prayers for the rising and the setting of the sun and many other daily experiences. The daily rhythms of their lives were always kept in the full light of their traveling with the Holy. The understanding of the imminent presence of God in such mundane tasks as washing the floor, milking the cows, building the fire that would warm them and cook their food, was never far from their lips, their heart. Some part of me longs to travel in such close Presence. How about you? From sunrise to sunset, through the profound moments of a full moon to the mundane of laundry, to remember that with every turning of

the day, the Holy and I make our path together. It is in the noticing that we come face to face with the truth. A truth to be remembered and claimed with the rising of each day.

Practice

Notice the rhythms of Creation today. Did you see the sun rise? Can you see the sun at its full height at noon? Are you in a place where you can see the sun make its final dip into the horizon? How can you honor the rhythms of this day?

Emerging Light

Yesterday morning, early, I sat in a chair looking out the window waiting for the day's light to emerge. I knew the lake was out there and that the ice houses had spent time in darkness being refrozen in place by the night's cold temperatures. During the day the balmy temps and glaring sun had created little moats around the tiny structures. But I trusted that the colder airs of nighttime had glued them safely once again to the lake's frozen surface. Blackness was all that I could see.

At some point of the night I had been awakened with the feeling that I had perhaps overslept. It was so light in my room, I thought it must be morning. But as I shook the sleep from my head and groped for consciousness, I saw it was the nearly full moon that was shining brightly through my window. I moved the pillows around in my retreat center bed and situated myself in the wash of its rays. It was a powerfully primal experience. Like those ancients who had known only the stars and moon as their canopy, I now found myself in their company. After some time, I must have fallen asleep once again, held in the waxing whiteness of the winter moon.

Hours layer I sat, waiting for the light to come once again to the morning sky. Slowly the blackness began to turn to a deep blue. The outlines of the enormous oak trees, naked in their February coats, slipped into the vision of the landscape. As the light emerged, shadows took form and I saw the tiny wooden houses become visible once again. I watched as the day began. I could now make out the cars and trucks parked beside the ice houses, confirming once again that there are people so much braver than I.

To watch a day arrive is a gift. I am happy to say that it was not a gift that was lost on me. I breathed in its pure possibility. I offered prayers for those things I believed the day would hold and also for those that would surprise me. Someplace, in the recesses of mind the scripture echoed: This is the day God has made. Rejoice!

And I felt the truth of that statement, and that command, at some very deep place within.

Practice

Today or sometime this week, set your alarm for the time the sun will rise. Keep your eyes on the day that is arriving. Ask for the grace to be present to both joy and sorrow and any surprises that come your way.

Holy Listening

Once again I find myself overlooking a frozen lake dotted with ice houses. It is February and time for a retreat in which a gathering of faithful people, some clergy and some not, will hear the stories of those who are coming to the United Methodist church to become ordained for ministry. It has been my privilege to serve in this way for several years now. In preparation for these interviews, we have read papers that have been prepared by the candidates and have watched sermons they have preached. But today we will do the truly holy work of speaking with them, asking questions, and entering the work of holy listening.

To begin our time together last night, we heard the story of Elijah, his love of God and telling God's movement in the world. Elijah is told to go out and stand on the mountain because the Holy One is about to pass by. In 1 Kings it says: *"Now there was a great wind, so strong that it was splitting mountains and breaking rocks in pieces before God, but God was not in the wind; and after the wind an earthquake; but God was not in the earthquake; and after the earthquake, a fire, but God was not in the fire; and after the fire, the sound of sheer silence."* The story goes on to say that when Elijah heard this powerful silence he covered his face and heard God's voice asking: "What are you doing here?"

I can imagine that at least a few of the candidates for ministry may have awoken this morning asking themselves this question. My prayer is that some small, still voice has entered them, allowing them to know that there are grace-filled people who are waiting to listen to their lives. My prayer is that they will know that we will be listening to the strong winds, the earthquakes, the fires, and, most importantly, the silences that have enfolded their journey.

This is why we are all here. This is the work for this day, for these people. But isn't this really the work we are offered every day? This is not the task set simply before

those who are interviewing people called to ministry. The work of holy listening is offered to us with the rising of the sun each day. In all our relationships. In all the daily comings and goings of work, family, play, in the errands we run, the strangers we encounter.

Earthquakes, strong winds, and fires are moving through the lives of nearly every person we meet. All these same acts are moving across the face of our world. Surely the Holy One is in it all. And there are those moments of sheer silence that also hold the gentle, sometimes prodding, presence of God. Our work, should we choose to accept it, is to practice holy listening. This is why we are here.

For the healing of the world . . .

Practice

Give yourself to listening this day. Listen to everyone you meet. Listen to the sounds of the world. Declare the listening you do, holy. God moves through you and all the sounds of this Creation.

What's in a Name?

On Friday, I indulged in some humidity therapy at the Como Conservatory. This has become a yearly winter pilgrimage timed just at the point when the dry skin which results from frigid days becomes unbearable. Friday seemed to be the near tipping point and I had a fairly open day ahead so it seemed a perfect thing to do.

Walking into the domed building, I was immediately hit with a rush of humid air. The sunglasses I had been wearing to protect myself against the glaring of sun off snow steamed up with a fog of moisture. I looked at those who were wearing regular glasses as we all stood just inside the doorway in a sort of limbo between sight and blindness. Their faces were bathed in smiles. Smiles of warmth, of heavy, moist air, of being surrounded by things that were alive . . . and green! We chuckled toward one another as we waited for the fog to melt off lenses.

These expeditions must always begin with a simple act of sitting down. Sitting down so you can allow your body to adjust to the instantaneous but beautiful assault of heavy, wet air and heat. After all, our bodies have been walking around in layers of fleece and wool for months. To all of a sudden walk into a tropical Eden takes some time of gentleness.

After the initial time of acclimation, I walked around, allowing the green ferns and plants and the colors and smells of the flowers to wash over me. Entering one of the smaller rooms, I found myself present to the Winter Carnival Orchid Show. The sheer beauty and color of these flowers was nearly overwhelming. But the best part came when I began to read the names of some of the unique varieties.

Staring at one orchid whose petals were larger than many of the others, I noticed its deep red, nearly purple flowerets. At its center was a rich, dark pink. Flecked across the petals themselves were little droplets of earthy yellows. The tag that identified the flower? Fine Wine. Well, of course it was. What else could it be?

I noticed some women looking up toward the ceiling at a pot that was suspended above our heads. At first I could not see anything but the slender green stems shooting out of a common terra cotta pot. But as my eyes searched further they beheld flashy hot pink circles of flower. Just on the edge of gaudy, these cascading blossoms looked like a feather boa falling gently off the neck of a lovely lady. Its name? Crown Fox Diva. Why was I not surprised?

But my personal favorite? Sitting quietly among all the other showy blooms, nestled back in the verdant plumage of all the other marvelous orchids sat Brother Buddha. Smaller more understated faces of brown centers hung gently from light green stems. The brown slowly gave way to a soft, dark pink until it finally emerged into the signature saffron of the robes of Buddhist monks. While not the most eye-catching of the orchid show, this plant seemed to know itself and be content with its gentle presence.

As I walked out of the room that housed the collection of the many-faceted orchids, I wondered about who named them. Whose job is it to watch these lovely creations and then name them with such accuracy? At that moment I longed for the privilege of such work. To name something, human or plant, is a great gift. Anyone who has ever looked into the face of a newborn, knowing they have the blessed power to attach syllables that will forever define a person's life, realizes it is something not to be taken lightly.

What is your name? How did it come to you? What is the story that accompanies your naming? In Genesis the task of naming was given to Adam, an awesome responsibility. From the very beginning of our sacred story, names have been important. Names like yours and mine. Names like Fine Wine and Crown Fox Diva and, especially, Brother Buddha.

Practice

Reflect on your name. What do you know about how you came to be named? Imagine how your life might have been different had you been named something else. Celebrate your name in some special way.

Face to Face

Over the last two days I have been in northern Minnesota at a clergy retreat. We were blessed to have been staying in a condo overlooking Lake Superior. To watch the play of light on the lake at various times of the day was a great gift. The coolness of color in the morning sun gave way to brilliance by noontime. As the sun began to sink farther into the horizon, the richness of the many possible shades of blue began to wash the sky.

Yesterday morning I was laying in my guest bed looking out at the morning sky as orange, peach, pink, and yellow wove a pattern resembling a swirling silk necktie along the horizon. I was laying there simply allowing this gift of color and silence to awaken me to another day. Out of the corner of my eye I saw a figure moving as if in slow motion, like a mime walking an imaginary tightrope. I moved to a seated position in the bed sitting cross-legged as in meditation. Not more than six feet from the sliding glass door of my room stood a deer looking straight into my watching eyes. Trying to imitate this creature's ability to stay still, I quieted my muscles and my breath until we were both simply being, looking at one another face to face. There was no fear in this wild creature who must know instinctively to fear humans. In that moment of staring into its beautiful, brown, unblinking eyes, I had the overwhelming feeling of being connected to a fellow creation in a deep way. It was a truly holy moment.

After several minutes of this encounter, the deer was joined by another, and they walked slowly off into the woods toward the lake. I wracked my brain trying to remember the Mary Oliver poem where she writes so beautifully about a similar experience. I cursed myself for not memorizing those poems I love so much, for not being able to pull them up at will for such a time as this. But then I gently realized that the experience I had just had perhaps needed no words to define it. It was simply a true moment of being.

Back home I went to the bookshelf to look for the poem. It is called "Five A.M. in the Pinewoods," and in it she describes what may have been a dream about an encounter with two deer or a real experience. Of course, the same could be said about my own encounter of these two brown-eyed creatures. Her words simply said them more succinctly, more beautifully.

Yes. I was looking for words to express my face-to-face encounter. I am glad to have found them. But what I am remembering are the beautiful, brown, unblinking eyes and the place they have made in my heart.

Practice

When have you had an encounter with an animal that was transforming or enlightening? Remember this experience. Give thanks for the gift of it.

Inhaling

Every now and then in the novels I read a sentence will jump out and find a home in me. Right now I am reading a beautifully written book called *Ahab's Wife or The Star Gazer* by Sena Jeter Naslund. It tells the many-layered life story of the wife of Ahab in another novel, *Moby Dick*. It is a story of the love of the sea that is fueled by a home in a lighthouse and one young woman's great courage to have a life of adventure and meaning. I highly recommend it.

A little more than a hundred pages into the book, one of the paragraphs begins: *"I went to the window to inhale the world."* When I read these words, a feeling of excitement swept over me. *"To inhale the world."* What a joyous and exhilarating thought! I thought to myself: "This is what I want to do." Everyday. And so as I continue to wade my way through this quite long book, I return often to the page whose corner I turned down, to remind myself of my own endeavor.

This morning I was blessed to wake up on the North Shore of Lake Superior. I opened my eyes to look out the window that overlooks the water to see the waxing moon shining through the leafless trees making a pathway of silver light on the frigid water. I lay in the warmth of my bed trying to inhale the sight, its beauty, its stillness. I allowed my lungs to fill deeply with the power of the scene. Inhale.

Breathing out the shard of a disturbing dream I had earlier, I breathed in the gift my window offered. The moon helped perspective float into my consciousness, and I felt grounded in the ever-turning goodness of Creation. Out on the lake the shimmering ice chunks moved about, driven by a current I cannot see but whose presence is known. The Spirit and the unseen current have much in common. I inhaled once again, allowing this truth to wash over me.

Of course, inhaling the world brings not only beauty and peace but also pain and uncertainty. To inhale the world I must see the fragile lives of people in turmoil

and in harm's way. It also means knowing the underbelly of a world often gone mad with greed, a world that forgets the intricate ways in which we are woven together—human . . . creature . . . soil . . . water . . . life.

To truly inhale the world, we must breathe in all of it. But that is really the beauty, isn't it? To be touched by the deep wonder and vulnerability of being alive means to embrace and inhale the fullness of all life has to offer. It is in those experiences when we come face to face with the Mystery of the One whose exhale brought us into being. It is in those moments when our grateful hearts find a connection we often name as prayer.

Out on the Big Lake the sun is showing its first light, spreading a show of pale pink against an even paler blue. I am standing at my window. Inhaling.

Practice

Sit in a quiet place where you can have a view of your world. Allow your eyes to drink in all of it. Inhale this world. Exhale all you need to release. Repeat.

Seal Skins

Yesterday I spend some time observing dozens of seals. I stood with nearly the same number of humans overlooking a cove in La Jolla, California, that is the resting spot of these amazing creatures. They lay nestled in the warm sand, their brown, gray, black, and speckled bodies sunbathing in the blazing light. Out on a large rocky area the seals were nearly invisible until the ocean water pounded over the sea wall, startling them from their basking. As the water shot out and over their rocky bed, the seals moved both their heads and tails to form the letter C. I think they might have been trying for the letter O but never quite made it.

On the softer, sandier ground, mother seals cradled small pups in the crooks of their bodies, warming them in safety. We watched as one small gray pup was nudged and prodded by the adult. Out into the water but not too far it went, closing monitored by the parent. What was going on here? A swimming lesson? At one point another adult seal got involved in the action, coming toward the tiny pup as if to add their own instructions. The mother seal turned quickly on the other adult, hissing and clearly pointing out who was boss. Talk about your Tiger Mom!

Nearby another mother lay sleeping, her somewhat older, maybe teenage pup snuggled near by. The younger seal was sleeping so soundly. I remember my own teenage sons sleeping this kind of sleep that cannot be disturbed by noise or movement. At one point the adult slowly opened her deep brown eyes, her lovely long eyelashes blinking toward me. We seemed to share a knowing look.

What amazing creatures seals are! Watching them yesterday, I thought of the ancient stories of selkies so prominent in Britain. Selkies, humans who had at one time been seals, were said to have come to land to become human, giving up their seal skins and often their souls as well, in an effort to become something other than who they were. Their stories are full of romance, melancholy, and often tragedy.

Watching the seals yesterday, I imagined early storytellers spinning the tale of those beings who came to live on land. The seals moved gracefully through the water, diving deep and coming up in places far from where they had begun. I can imagine those land-livers with vivid flights of fancy wanting to be able to do such wild and amazing acts, and creating stories that would merge the life of land and sea. But observing the seals while on land was something completely different. It seemed neither their front flippers nor their back ones were quite strong enough to move any distance. Here their movements were instead clumsy and labored, almost painful to observe.

As I watched these endearing creatures, I thought of all those who want to be something other than what they are. Many of us wish to embrace the wildness and grace of the seals in the sea. And at the same time we wish to have the assurance of the ground beneath our feet. There are sacrifices inherent in both. Often we give up great parts of ourselves without weighing all the odds. The selkie was often seen standing on shore looking out toward a life that had once been, unable to find the skin that would have allowed them to swim with grace once again. They had lost their uniqueness and were not able to go home.

Today I am thankful to these beautiful beings for all the gifts they offer. The gifts of awe, beauty, joy, grace, and even mystery. As a land-living storyteller I was also blessed with the reminder to honor being comfortable in my own skin and to celebrate the unique and diverse beings with which I share this path of Creation.

Practice

Spend time looking at your skin. Note all the freckles, spots, lines that are you. Offer gratitude for all your skin does for you, how it protects you.

Scent Memory

For the sense of smell, almost more than any other, has the power to recall memories and it is a pity we use it so little. – RACHEL CARSON

I find myself surrounded by incredible scents. We have just arrived in San Diego for a few days of vacation and time with family. As quickly as our legs would take us upon our arrival at the airport, we walked outside to just smell the warm, moist air. The ocean was not far off, our noses told us. As our eyes took in the green grass and the swaying palm trees, we were also flooded with a wash of flowery scents. It was a delight after so many months of frigid, sterile Midwestern air. And so I have found myself walking up to nearly every green and blossoming plant, not only drinking in the color, but absorbing the richness of scent. Ahhhh . . .

It is said that our sense of smell is most tied to memory. Most recently I was walking through a store and got the overwhelming sense of my grandmother who died over twenty years ago. I still don't know what the smell was, but it was some mix of flowery sweetness that sent me back to times snuggled safely in her tiny house as we sat at a card table tackling the challenge of a jigsaw puzzle. The scent of memory has the power to conjure up so many experiences.

I recall a conference I attended many years ago on the subject of the spirituality of children. The opening ritual invited those in attendance to share their earliest memory of worship. I was struck with the memories of those whose traditions involved the sense of smell—sweet oil, incense, candles. Their memories were described in rich detail and represented experiences of a much earlier age than those whose tradition had abandoned these worship practices. I remember feeling sad that my own tradition had, over the years, been stripped of these scent-filled rituals.

And yet I perhaps will never smell the perfume Evening in Paris (Do they still make this?) without thinking of worship services in my little church in southern Ohio.

Positioned between my mother and my brothers, I could smell the exotic, fruity scent of my mother's perfume wafting in the humid, heavy air. My father's Old Spice aftershave was no doubt filling my brother's head with equally tranquilizing thoughts. These scents were not created for liturgical practices, but they provided the backdrop for the scripture and prayers of our tradition to be seeded in our hearts and minds. These seemingly elegant smells relegated to dress-up clothes and special occasions were not the scents of our everyday. Combined with the peppermints we were secretly handed from the hidden treasure chest of my mother's purse, we were kept quiet and attentive in worship by perfume and candy. Though not traditional elements of worship, they make up my sense memory to this day.

The power of our sense of smell gets neglected during Minnesota winters. But as the snow continues to melt and the Earth once again comes to life before our eyes and under our noses, the memories of experiences planted deep within us will float to the forefront. They are to be celebrated and honored for the gifts they continue to offer. Gifts of the present and also days long gone by.

Today I will continue to add to the my bank of scent memory. The native Californians may notice a woman stopping to smell every colorful flower she sees. Like the humming bird I saw yesterday hovering over the red flowers of an azalea bush, I will be collecting. Collecting the memories of scent to store away for another winter when I will need their sweetness and their assurance of life renewed.

Practice

Open yourself to the sense of smell. Notice the exotic and the ordinary. Store these smells for the times you need them most.

Goose Blessing

This morning was as busy as most. I had been bustling around the house making piles of things I needed to bring into church—magazines, soup, the bag with my computer, my purse. It didn't help that I had slept in later than usual. Before I could make it to the office, I had several errands I needed to run for our Wednesday evening Lenten supper and gathering. I had made a couple of trips to load the car and was on my last exit out the door carrying a crockpot of hot soup for tonight's pot luck when I was greeted with a sound from the sky.

Overhead, flying quite low a gaggle of geese were making their way home. In their perfect "V" formation they swept across the morning sky with spirit and intention. Nestled in the formation was one lone goose. It almost made the letter "A" with its body! Only the sound of air being cut by wings echoed in the frosty blueness of the day. And then one single "Honk!" I stopped in my tracks. My bustling came to a halt, and I was royally chastised by this goose blessing. These beautiful winged signs of spring put me in my place simply by doing what they knew how to do: make their way toward home.

You see, in my pursuit to get all the things checked off my daily list, I had forgotten to be alive to the world, had forgotten to be awake to the sun glistening off the remaining icicles on the neighbor's house. I had forgotten to notice the green grass emerging from under piles of dirty, tired snow. I had forgotten to be grateful for the gift of another precious day. I had forgotten my true home.

And then the geese flew over and jarred me out of my numbness. They blessed me with memory. As they used their inner resources to find their way home, they announced their place in the family of things. They also reminded me of mine.

And so the question has flown with me all day, does this mean that spring is *really* on its way?

Practice

What sound wakes you up to yourself? What signal calls you home? Is there a way to replicate and reproduce this sound as a sacred reminder?

Glory Everywhere

Beyond Easter,
we go singing.
Having been grabbed
by resurrections
we are full of tears and laughter.
The way ahead is unknown.
It will always be like that.
But having danced in the light
we will look for glory everywhere.
– RUTH BURGESS

An interesting coincidence is that in 2011 the Christian observance of Good Friday and the international observance of Earth Day fell on the same day. I have been thinking about how these particular observances might inform one another. For Christians, Good Friday commemorates the crucifixion of Jesus. It is a somber day, one where introspection, repentance, and penitence is offered. Earth Day was created to help us be reminded of the ways in which we humans who call Earth home do so in a daily act of interdependence. We do this not only with our fellow humans but also with all living things—animals, plants, water, air, soil. We are all connected in ways unknown and known to us.

For those who made their way to a worship service on that day, they read the scriptures of how Jesus entered Jerusalem only to be arrested, tried, and sentenced to death. His ministry had been about building communities that were healing, compassionate, just, and moved with hope. This work, his presence, was a great threat to the power structures, structures which worked to keep people in need, under control, alienated from one another and from their own sense of power.

Our Earth home is being threatened by a mindset and systems that deny the innumerable ways we are bound together in our common life. Clean water, healthy air, and nutrient rich soil are being killed off. Our burning desire and addiction to fossil fuels continues to bring both economic and political hardship. The issues sometimes threaten to overwhelm the most rational among us. And so Earth Day also calls for introspection, repentance, and penitence.

But what kept the disciples going and what can keep us going in the face of what sometimes seems nearly impossible to hold is the important fact that we have seen new life happen again and again and again. Devastated people work to pull themselves out of the aftermath of disasters; they continue to show remarkable signs of hope as they reach out to one another and employ immense creativity to solve huge problems. As a nation many among us are continuing to chip away at systems that do not take the Earth into consideration. Many are offering creative alternatives for living "with" rather than simply "on" the planet.

Like Jesus' ministry, like the disciples' work that followed and continues today, it is slow work. Work that is often misunderstood and threatening. But it is work that continues to lift before an often blind and battered people: We must depend on one another. We must take care for the good of all. It is what we were born to do, to be.

For me the sure way of reminding myself of this claim on my life is to "look for glory everywhere" as the writer Ruth Burgess says. When I am attuned to the glory that comes to me as pure gift, I am reminded of my responsibility, of all the many invisible lines of connection that make up my life, my living. I travel this world with the story of Jesus planted deep within me. I also travel its whirling paths on a planet that continues to fill my lungs with air, nourish me with water and food. I travel with companions that delight and surprise me with beauty and wonder. Indeed, glory is everywhere when I have eyes to see.

Good Friday. Earth Day. So many connections to honor. So many opportunities to be a part of the on-going telling of goodness in the world. What a privilege! What a responsibility.

Practice

Make note of the glory around you. Celebrate the goodness this glory brings to you and to the world. Offer your prayers of gratitude.

Trickster

Easter Sunday brought with it the glorious weather for which we have been longing. Sunshine and warm temperatures illuminated everyone's Easter finery. People wore big smiles as they greeted one another. Children could be seen in various yards and parks hunting for brightly colored eggs hidden in obvious sight in the still greening grass. It was indeed a beautiful day.

I began the morning with our Easter sunrise service. It is one of my favorite worship experiences of the year. There is always something mysterious and exciting about getting to church in the dark, watching others arrive with sleep still hanging on them, to do something a little out of the ordinary. And this year's service certainly delivered that experience.

Just as we were beginning the service, I walked outside to prop the door open for the grand entrance of one of our guest musicians who would be playing the didgeridoo, that wonderful Australian instrument whose tones touch something deep and primal in us. A few people were entering at the last minute and we all were surprised, shocked actually, to see a coyote walking across the lawn and parking lot near the church entrance. That's right, a coyote! In the middle of the city, only hundreds of feet away from a major freeway entrance ramp.

It was such a shock we hardly knew how to react. Many thoughts went quickly through my head. Where did it come from? How did it get this far into the city without being injured or even killed by all the speeding cars and trucks? How was it going to find its way to safety? My colleague who lives next to the church pointed out that a family of rabbits lives near his house. My mind then raced to the rabbits and their safety. All these thoughts flew through my brain as we began our sunrise worship.

As I welcomed the people to our Easter morning together, I shared the coyote sighting. Heads shifted in wonder and surprise. Then someone said loudly: " Ah, the trickster!" Indeed, in the Native American stories of the Southwest, the coyote is seen as the trickster who comes to shake things up, to help the people see things in new ways. After doing a little research I read that in one myth the coyote also brings seeds of life to sow new growth upon the new world. Interesting.

Perhaps this relative of the dogs we love so much was simply a misplaced animal who had wandered too far into the urban chaos. All I know is that his presence caused many of us to take quick, surprised breaths, to sit up more attentively in our seats, to be open to what other gifts the day might dish up. Easter morning had provided an experience we had not rehearsed. Even those who had not actually seen the coyote with their own eyes told others about what they had heard. Much like the women in the gospel story we read in the hour that unfolded after the coyote sighting, people continued to tell the story of this strange and startling vision. We all carried into the day the message of surprise, confusion, new life.

If coyote is a trickster, I think on this Sunday his work was a trick of the best kind. And I pray, now that his work is done, that he has found a safe place to make his home.

Practice

What needs to be shaken up in your life? Who or what is acting as trickster for you? Be open and present to all the surprises that come your way which may lead to the newness that is unfolding.

Rising

The dead shall rise again
whoever says
dust must be dust
don't see the trees
smell rain
remember africa
everything that goes
can come
stand up
even the dead shall rise.
– LUCILLE CLIFTON, *The Raising of Lazarus*

I woke this morning to snow falling outside the window. The trees once again are wearing a glistening coat of white looking like a scene held captive by the White Witch from C.S. Lewis' book, *The Lion, The Witch and the Wardrobe*. I was reminded of the first Easter I lived in Minnesota, seeing the little girls in their springy dresses and hats, their little white shoes shuffling through the equally white, slushy snow. I want to believe that Easter fell much earlier in the year than this one, but I could be wrong.

Even though the snow might douse our spirits today, I am making the commitment to keep my mind on what is being reborn. Our garden is a visual reminder. Tulips, irises, and other early bloomers are undaunted as they make their green way into the world once again after being held in darkness and cold for so many months. The lovely little warbler that snuggled in the branches of a tree outside our living room window this morning is another. He had the same dazed look we did as we watched the flakes falling. I saw an earthworm wriggling on the pavement trying to make his way to the now-thawed ground, ready to do the work he is created to do.

There are also people I know who are experiencing a kind of rebirth after what seemed like a slow walk through a dark valley. Those who have known the full throttled pain and uncertainty of illness are now on the other side of despair, filled with a hope they thought might be lost forever. Still others have moved through painful job and relationship conflicts and are arriving at new places of understanding and commitment. What seemed like never-ending dust has become something that is breathing new life. This is the wheel of life at its full spin.

Some spring seasons simply take longer to grow into their fullness. This spring is one of them. Just like some of us who need more patient nurture and support, this spring is inching into existence at its own labored tempo. And yet, by day's end the snow will likely be melted and gone into the on-going process of watering the sore earth. As humans short on patience, our work is to watch and wait and notice the tiny glimpses of new life wherever we see them.

And in our noticing we can take a moment to be grateful. Very, very grateful. Snow falls. Snow melts. But a grateful heart is something to hold onto for dear life.

Practice

Plant some seeds today, literal or otherwise. Seeds of kindness, goodness, hope. Water and nurture them well for the growth that is yet to come.

In Cahoots

It could be said that God's foot is so vast
that the entire earth is but a
field on God's toe,
and all the forests in this world
came from the same root of just
a single hair
of the Holy.
What then is not sanctuary?
Where then can I not kneel
and pray at a shrine
made holy by God's
presence? – ST. CATHERINE OF SIENA

During my Saturday morning trip to the farmer's market this week, I had a realization that filled me with awe and humility. As I walked the rows of colorful flowers and fragrant herbs, I had this overwhelming feeling of connection with both those who sold their wares and those, like me, who were doing the shopping. As I handed my money to the beautiful Hmong woman whose head was wrapped in a brilliant blue and red patterned scarf and she, in turn, handed me my rhubarb, I knew we were in this thing together. I listened to the laughter of the tall, blond farmer, dressed in bibbed overalls as if in costume, selling honey and humor. As his voice washed over me, I had the full-bodied sense that we were all in cahoots with one another in this journey called life. I looked at my fellow shoppers and saw, not strangers, but family caring for the very basic need of all creatures. The need to eat.

Now this may seem to some a lot to hang on the simple act of shopping at the farmer's market. But it was truly one of those full-bodied realizations that comes to us every now and then. One of those feelings of recognition that we are a small part of a much larger, intricate, and beautiful whole. I thought of the work that these farmers had done on our behalf. The planning, the planting, the watering, the weeding, the watching, and the eventual harvesting. All the shoppers were there to reap the rewards of the work of others. And while money was exchanged for services rendered, it seemed much more than that.

It was a reminder to me of all those who labor so my life, and yours, may be lived. All those who work unseen to make sure my lights turn on when I flip a switch and the heat goes on when I press a button. All those who drive trucks and trains and planes to bring other goods for my use and consumption. It is staggering when you think about it. All the lives that are attached to ours through their work. It is a fact that could, and should, humble us if we let it.

The truth is we are all in cahoots to live this life. We can move through the world acting as if we are independent and self-sufficient but the reality is that very few, if any, can live our lives without the work and toil of others. The very idea fills me with such a deep sense of gratitude and joy and humility. It becomes, for me, an image of this huge family that travels with me wherever I go. We are kin of the living kind, depending on one another, looking out for one another, supporting one another, always full of the realization that when one rejoices we all rejoice and when one grieves we all grieve.

At the farmer's market I was happy to look across the sea of faces and notice how different we all looked. Different body shapes, a myriad of skin colors, some old and wrinkled and others new to the world, and yet all kin. All joined together for that moment in the pursuit of good food. Food offered to us by hands that had known the soil that would feed us all. In that moment it seemed to me not only an act of Creation but also an act of communion.

Thanks be to God.

Practice

Pay attention to every morsel of food you eat this day. Imagine the path it took to get to your plate, to your mouth. Imagine the many hands that made your meal possible. Say grace for this holy meal.

Heron

The Twin Cities' area is still looking over its shoulder after the tornadoes that ripped through North Minneapolis on a Sunday afternoon. Friends who live near there have spoken of the devastation and the sadness of seeing many who were already living on the economic edge now dealing with no roof, no power, needing help with services many of us take for granted. While nowhere near as destructive as the storms in Missouri, these hurts close to home have held our thoughts, our prayers. They also have reminded many of us about the power of perspective as we take stock of the ups and downs of our days.

We certainly know that when storms of this magnitude move through any populated area, the damage does not fall on humans alone. We are, after all, a part of an intricately woven Creation. To see the trees that were uprooted and split along block after block is a gentle reminder that these are homes, too. Home to birds and animals, all as fragile and as easily displaced as humans.

This morning I read about the heron rookery that existed on one of the lakes in the path of the storm's winds. Several dozen great blue herons called these trees home. In those trees were nests, each holding two or three young herons, fresh and new to the world. After the storm, the mature herons, their strong deep blue wings soaring, were seen circling overhead looking for their young, for a sign of their former homes. What a tragic sight that must have been!

I thought of my favorite poet, Mary Oliver, who has written so often about the beautiful herons she has observed in her many years as a poet and lover of all that lives. Her poem, simply entitled "Heron," reminds us of the importance of noticing, of not being so caught up in our humanness that we forget there are teachers without words. I commend the poem to you.

Those interviewed in the paper who know about herons and other ones with wings, seemed less troubled than I was at their plight. They spoke of how the herons are survivors and will continue to live out their summer life and will make their way back to this place next spring. The fallen trees, they reminded, will now become home to other birds who make their homes closer to the ground, nearer to the water. The herons will rebuild their nests and begin again. It is the way it works. These "servants of the system" understand perhaps things we in our city mentalities do not. They will cast their pure light on what is yet to be.

Unlike the herons, humans may find it difficult to see much past the devastation at this point. I do know that there are countless people who, at this very moment, are carrying food and water, chopping up fallen trees and hauling debris, reaching out to neighbors whose names they had not known before the storm moved through. Within hours, people were collecting money to fuel the work that needs to be done. Prayers were said and continue to float in the air, hovering over the streets and blue tarps that act as roofs, much like the outstretched wings of the herons over the rookery.

Pure light. Pure light.

Practice

What disaster needs prayer and pure light? Light a candle, shed light, and offer a wide-winged prayer for all those who suffer.

Melting

For several months now I have been keeping watch over a strange, and somewhat marvelous, sight. Nearly every day for the last seven months as I make my way onto the freeway entrance ramp near the Cathedral in St. Paul, I glance over at the Sears parking lot. The lot has been home to an enormous mound of snow. At its peak it was, I would guess, several stories tall and larger than two rambler houses set end to end. Next to this mound was a smaller but still impressive mound of frozen precipitation. Over the last two to three months these formations have lost their whiteness and instead have become black and grimy with exhaust, pollution, and just good, old, normal dirt.

The thing is, it is now May 18 and the snow hills are still there! That's right. It has been at least eighty degrees on a couple of days and in the sixties and seventies the last couple of weeks. Still, snow sits on the Sears lot. It has slowly shrunk to perhaps ten feet in height, and a small trickle of melted water makes its way onto the boulevard. But there is still snow on the ground here in St. Paul.

While I can and do take varying routes to the office, I now have been going only one way. It has become a daily ritual to check on "my" snow. The sight of it makes me laugh and reminds me from where we've come. And as I've observed this near glacier like movement of melt, its presence has become metaphor for me.

The enormous mound of snow has come to represent all that which builds up in our lives and becomes bigger than its individual parts. When I think of the size of a snowflake, each with individual beauty and uniqueness, I am humbled. When those same snowflakes get piled on top of one another for hours, days, weeks, months, they become something very different. Something that lasts a very long time. Something that gets covered with dirt and garbage which, then, forms a crust that makes it nearly impenetrable. The fragility of snowflakes held together is a profound and powerful statement.

That is what has happened to the Sears snow. That is what also happens to us when hurts and grudges are allowed to pile up and cement themselves to our souls. It is what happens when we find ourselves encrusted with bad habits, hurtful words, addictions, old baggage we allow to define us. The pile gets higher and higher, and it takes a powerful force to melt its hold. Ever have this happen in your life?

What can melt such a structure? The warmth of friendship and community is a good start. Self-loving also helps. Asking and seeking forgiveness goes a long way. Being gentle with ourselves and others can be helpful. Recognizing what is ours to do and not do is also powerful. Prayer. Laughter. A good cup of coffee and a piece of chocolate wouldn't hurt either.

I'll make my way to the office in a few minutes. As I drive by the snow that lingers into May, I'll laugh. Laugh and offer my thanks for its gifts and the wisdom it has offered.

I'll also pray that it melts very soon.

Practice

Place an ice cube in a glass or shallow bowl. As it melts, offer the things in your own life that need letting go. When the ice has become water, use it to give moisture to a living thing.

Awe-Struck

Such love does
The sky now pour
That whenever I stand in a field,
I have to wring out the light
When I get home.
— ST. FRANCIS OF ASSISI

It is rare these days when the newspaper gives over precious print space on the editorial pages for something other than acerbic political or intentionally divisive writing. But yesterday there was an editorial that caught my eye and had me saying "Amen" under my breath long before breakfast. The title of the article was Shocked at what passes for awe these days," and it was written by two professors at Normandale Community College. The general message of the writers was that, as a people, we have become immune to awe, that we are a people fulfilling important responsibilities but who are uninspired. All the while, they say, we also long to be awestruck.

Perhaps I was drawn to this article because I share their opinion, their concern. I have long believed that the environmental crisis in which we find ourselves is fueled by our inability to connect at a deep level with awe for the Creation that holds us. When I read the psalms, many reflecting the sheer power of a call to an awe-filled life, I am humbled by the ancient poets' ability to send up their full-bodied celebration of awe: The awe they experiences at Creation and its intricate patterns and beautiful, powerful creatures. The inspiration that grounds them as those whose work seems to be to shout that praise to the world. If this were our common experience of the beautiful, fragile world in which we live, how could we do anything to harm it for ourselves or for those who will come after? Too often those who tell the cautionary tales of climate change do so only with facts and figures, leaving out the call to an awe-filled life.

When have you experienced awe lately? When has some moment of your day taken your breath away? When was the last time you felt goosebumps or found your eyes welling up at the beauty or wonder of some encounter? The opportunities for being awe-inspired, I believe, have not decreased in our world. We have simply chosen to live the distracted life that keeps us from being awake to all the myriad ways awe is jumping up and down saying," See me! See me!"

The psalmists of ancient days took the time to watch the sunrise, to gaze at the mountain formations, to watch the stag drink from a glistening stream. They allowed this experience of the Holy to wash over them and remind them they that were a part of something greater than their small, finite life. Then they shaped their words and told their story. Are we called to do anything less?

We each wake up every morning with the potential to be awestruck at nearly very turn. The choice is ours as we walk out into the world. We can spend the day ticking off the items on our lists that have no end. Or we can choose to have an encounter with Mystery. We can notice the deep blue of the eyes of the person who hands us our morning coffee. We can stop to watch the pink crabapple blossoms fall slowly, like a baptism, over the woman standing at the bus stop. (I was witness to such a scene just yesterday.) We can take a moment to gaze into the center of the nearly spent tulips. How is that brilliant star shape at the center even possible? We can notice the gently arcing eyebrows of the baby that passes us on the sidewalk. We can stare at the soft wrinkles of the hands of the elderly woman who is recounting her recent aches and pains. What love and tenderness have these hands known? We can listen to the orchestra of bird songs outside the window and marvel at a language we will never speak.

Awe. It is all around us. Like St. Francis, who gave his life to living simply in the wonder and mystery of his time, we too can arrive at the end of our day needing to wring out the light that has bathed us.

And wouldn't that be a wonderful way to live a life? And wouldn't that be a wonderful way to begin healing the world?

Practice

Choose to give yourself to awe this day. Keep a running list of the ways in which you encounter the miraculous and mysterious wonders in the course of the everyday. Consider writing a psalm in praise of what you experienced.

Potting Soil

God said, "Let the earth grow plant life; plants yielding seeds and fruit trees bearing fruit with seeds inside it, each according to its kind throughout the earth." And that's what happened.

– GENESIS 1:11

It is a rare person who, these days, is not thinking of planting, of growing things, of soil to be turned and seeds to be burrowed. Even those who would not think of doing any actual gardening are aware of the Earth making a stupendous come-back in these evolving days of spring. In Minnesota the past two days seemed to have taken a giant leap forward into summer with temperatures in the eighties. But we know that in a few days things will be back on track and the slow, methodical opening of buds and sowing of seeds will resume.

It is easy to believe that this is the way it always is. But anyone who has planted any kind of plant or garden at anytime knows that most growing happens in its own good time, under circumstances that often elude the most skillful gardener. I can't even consider the number of dollars we have spent on our backyard garden, trying to make things grow, until we recognized that the black walnut trees we loved so much created a soil which makes many things impossible to grow. We had to accept that, if we loved the strength and the shade and the beauty of these trees, we had to give up growing certain plants. We had to accept the potting soil that is our yard.

Many times I engage in what I refer to as "wicked step-sister" behavior. I try with all my might to jam my foot—or myself—into a shoe or situation that simply doesn't fit. I cannot accept that I can't grow in every setting. I don't think I am alone in this, am I? I also often forget that sometimes the *not* blooming, *not* growing, *not* flowering may also be a path to a newer awareness of God's movement in my life and may lead to a wisdom I cannot learn in any other way.

In addition to this personal life realization, it has also been one of the most difficult lessons, I believe, of being a parent. To trust that your children will blossom in their own ways and not in the ways in which you had planned for them, is an often humbling journey. To accept the mystery of their path and yours in relationship to them is one of those lessons that often needs to be learned over and over again. I know I have certainly done my fair share of returning to the wisdom of that kind of potting soil.

For those who are struggling with a gardening diagram that may not be producing the blooms you had hoped. For those who are having difficulty accepting what is or isn't growing in your life right now. For all those who wake every day unsure of the next step, may you, may I, continue to accept ourselves and one another with the compassion and love offered by the Holy One. May we continue to dig deep into this potting soil and begin to grow in ways that may seem strange . . . but always mysterious.

Practice

Reflect on your life, its ebb and flow, its ups and downs. What have been the sources of your growth? What has helped you to move to the next step on your path?

Scripture and Verse

One of the rewards of taking public transportation is that you are reminded of the ways in which we are all so intricately woven together as people. When I have the gift of taking the light rail commuter train, I find myself jostled and soothed by the variety of people around me and the rhythm of its movement. On beautiful mornings like I experienced today, you get the added advantage of looking out the window and seeing the city you love fly by in a flash of speed and color. This vision was accompanied on this particular morning by the sound of a young woman sitting beside me quietly speaking a language I did not know into her cell phone. Those with bicycles loaded on and off flanked by fashionable men and women in business clothes: suits, ties, skirts, black high-heeled shoes. Nearly every person carried a backpack or briefcase that held items that remain a mystery to their fellow riders. Only the imagination tells the story of their work, their life.

Once off the train a vast array of people walked toward offices or buses or wherever their day might take them. There were also those that have no destination. Their day most likely consisted of trying to find their next meal, a helping hand, or a place to sleep the night. The diversity of faces and clothing told a part of the story but not its fullness. This kind of imaginative jogging is why I love to be able to use this mode of getting to work. It is not lost on me that this way of travel is a choice and not a necessity for me. My ability to spin stories and observe people's lives represents my privileged life.

Last night as I made my way toward the train that would take me to my waiting car, I observed many interesting sites. But the one that stuck with me throughout the evening and into this morning was the street preacher that had taken his stand on Nicollet and Eighth Street. Standing on a metal platform no wider than a kitchen ladder, he held a small, hand-lettered sign that simply read "Fear God." He was expounding with some effort about all the ways in which we are meant to fear

God, using scripture to back it up. But he was not a polished speaker nor a learned student of the Bible. He looked down periodically at his 3x5 white note cards to get his next scripture citation.

"For the wages of sin is death. Romans 6:23," he spoke, checking his note card. He then went on to say how we are all sinners and that is why we should fear God. As I waited for the light to turn, I found myself watching and listening out of a sense of obligation and identification. You see, I am not very good at being able to cite scripture . . . chapter and verse . . . either, so I felt a kinship with him. And while I don't agree with him theologically, I was also humbled by his courage to stand out in public and put his faith out there for all to see.

Sharing the same corner soap box were two young people signing people up for Amnesty International. Perhaps they, too, were putting their faith out there. I watched them NOT watch the street preacher. Their eyes instead were on an inebriated young man who was sitting on the ground in front of them. A security guard was trying to get him to his feet urging him to "be mature about this." Frankly, it was a lot of life to cram into a few square feet of concrete.

The light changed, and I was forced to leave this little drama being played out. I did not walk on "fearing" God anymore than I did on any other day. This preacher's sermon was lost on me. But what I was captured by was his commitment and the commitment of the Amnesty International volunteers. And I was held by compassion for the young man who had too much to drink and the one who was trying to help him without causing a scene or inciting violence.

In that scene, a snapshot really of any given moment on any given day on God's Creation, I was struck by "awe." Awe at the frailty and the courage of humans. Awe at the ways in which a moment can connect us in ways that startle and break our hearts. You see, "awe" is the true meaning of the words in scripture we have come to translate as "fear." The scriptures urge us to be in awe before God, not to be afraid of God.

For a few moments on an ordinary Monday on a little plot of sidewalk, I knew the depth of what it means to stand in awe before God.

Practice

Can you quote any particular scripture? Is there a poem you have committed to memory? Find one verse or line of a poem that you want to remember and be able to hang on to. Memorize it.

Investment

A few weeks ago I took a little trip to Savannah, Georgia, with my mother. It was a wonderful drive through mountains green with hardwood trees that in just a few weeks will paint a palette along the roadways with swashes of red, orange, and gold. As we drove along, we imagined what a sight that will be.

Once in the lovely city of Savannah, we took a trolley ride around the city as we learned some of the city's history and horticulture. At one point we turned a corner near Forsythe Park and learned of a very special tree. The enormous Candler Oak stands sentinel over this beautiful park from a lonely spot on a parking lot near a hospital that has been long closed. The story told by our guide recounted a failed development deal between some New York builders who wanted buy the empty hospital and put up housing. The catch? The 300-year-old tree would have to go. The people of Savannah said ,"No way," and the building still sits empty.

It was a wonderful story, and I hope it is true. The idea that, in these modern times, any group of people would forgo such an economic deal for the love of a tree warms my heart. As we passed the towering tree, I have to admit to feeling a deep emotion stir within me, and I can't get the image of that magnificent tree out of my mind. To what has this tree been present over these three centuries? Wars? Romances? Children growing? People aging? Who has stood, as I did, giving thanks for its strong trunk, its sheltering branches? Just imagine the life, and the changes in lives, that have been witnessed by this giant oak.

Tonight while searching through some worship resources, I read these words of Howard Thurman:

> *When the storms blew, the branches of the large oak in our backyard would snap and fall. But the utmost branches of the oak tree would sway just enough to save themselves from snapping loose. I needed the strength of that tree, and, like it, I*

wanted to hold my ground. Eventually, I discovered that the oak tree and I had a unique relationship. I could sit, my back against its trunk, and feel the same peace that would come to me in my bed at night. I could reach down in the quiet places of my spirit, take out my bruises and my joys, unfold them, and talk about them. I could talk aloud to the oak tree and know that I was understood.

Perhaps those who made the decision to rule, not in the favor of progress, but for the life of this oak, understood what it means to "need the strength of a tree." In their decision to save this glorious gift of Creation, they made an investment. An investment in relationship. An investment in quiet places, in spirit, in peace, and in healing.

The tree, at 300 years, cannot stand forever. But those who chose to let the tree live, to stand their ground, have provided an example of things that matter for the long haul. Hopefully, that has made all the difference, not only for this mighty oak, but for all who choose to learn from its story.

Practice

What gift of creation brings strength to you? If not a tree, what sight in the natural world helps ground you and help you find yourself again? Make a date with this strength-giver and yourself.

Fair Prayer

Many of us who aren't farmers or gardeners still have some element of farm nostalgia in our family past, real or imagined: a secret longing for some connection to a life where a rooster crows in the yard.

BARBARA KINGSOLVER, *Animal, Vegetable, Miracle: A Year of Food Life*

We have reached a pivotal time in the life-cycle of a year. Those of us who have gardens are being held in the grip of bounty. A friend said to me just the other day that she needed to head home and make something for supper that included tomatoes. Otherwise, the balance would tip and the tomatoes would overtake the human capacity to deal with them. This morning's trip to the St. Paul Farmer's Market was a testament to this pivotal time. The bright reds and greens of summer produce sat alongside apples and squash, a herald of the autumn abundance that is just around the corner.

And of course, the Minnesota State Fair began a few days ago. This yearly homage to all things Minnesotan is a delight to many and a necessary evil to others. But no matter your feelings about the State Fair, it is clearly an opportunity to connect with the bounty, both beautiful and bizarre, that the earth can produce. This morning when I read this prayer meant to be a table grace, I thought of my own experience of the fair.

You see, when I attend this annual extravaganza, I am not attracted to the thrill of rides or the kitschy trinkets found along the midway. I am not even attracted by the chance to rub elbows with local celebrities or politicians. From the moment I enter the gates I am aware of all the many ways this is a place to showcase what has been brought to fruition by hard work, creativity, collaboration, innovation, and a big dose of humor. This is all held together with a sense of sacrifice. Sacrifice

of resources, time, and even ego on the part of the humans. Anything grown or fed from the Earth is a practice in remembering that none of us acts independently. Sacrifice of energy, rain, soil, nutrients on the part of Creation provide gifts which are less easy to find a listening ear to offer our gratitude.

When I see row upon row of prize-winning vegetables, the enormous pumpkins, the deep purple eggplants, the perfectly formed green beans, I am moved nearly to tears by the notion of all that went into their being present before my eyes. Gazing on all the handmade pies, cakes, canned goods, and artwork, I am overwhelmed by all the hands that have offered their work for my inspiration and enjoyment. Watching the young people show their animals—sheep, goats, pigs, cattle, horses—I think of the countless hours logged to raise these creatures who have been nurtured since birth by hopeful hands and loving hearts. No doubt much human energy and care has been poured into seeing this animal walk into a pen, far from home, to be judged by people who are knowledgeable in ways beyond my comprehension.

Visiting the State Fair provides a wide angle lens to what is the microscopic lens with which we usually live our daily lives. The lens shows us that we are intricately woven together with others we will never meet. Sustained by forces we cannot see or understand. At home in a Universe that demands our dependence upon one another. Held in a dancing balance by the Spirit.

And so I send prayers of gratitude to all that has given of itself this day. For the warming and vitalizing sun, the nourishing earth and refreshing waters, the transforming fires, I offer my thanks. May this pivotal time of year find me remembering all the hands that have tended my food and my life. May this memory be present not just for a few days at the end of the summer, but every day.

Blessed be.

Practice

Take time to offer grace before all meals this day. And not just meals, but the cup of coffee and the glass of water. Connect your gratitude with a Universe that offers itself to you.

Growing? Coping?

Occasionally daily bits of wisdom are parceled out to me through my daily horoscope. This past week's words caught my attention at the breakfast table. It read: "Are you growing or merely coping? You make so much happen in a day (and so much happens to you, as well) that you can't help but wonder when the sun is setting how it's all adding up." So much for a trivial beginning to a regular Thursday. Instead I was offered big questions to help shape what I thought was going to be just an ordinary day. The horoscope seemed significant, so I tore it out and threw it into my purse.

Growing? Or simply coping? Are you ever plagued by this conundrum? Of course, every morning most of us wake up with the pure intention of growing, of blossoming beyond belief for the whole world to see. But the truth of the matter is that all those things we might make happen or that might happen to us often result in mostly coping. It can find us at the setting of the sun wondering what we did do with the precious hours, minutes, and seconds that were offered to us. How did we remember to breathe in the goodness that came our way? How did we keep our hearts open to acts of compassion that brushed up against our broken spirits? What were the moments of simplicity that reached out to grab our deepest longings? When did we allow the eyes behind our eyes to take a snapshot that might last a lifetime?

Often the intention with which we begin each day most often gets overshadowed by invisible threads, pieces of lint, and bits of paper that make up the pile with which we end the day. Have you ever had the experience of finding yourself unable to remember what actually happened during large sections of a day that is just ending? I find this to be quite unnerving and a sure sign that I may be in a coping rather than a growing mode.

What is growing in your life? Summer is so full of growth. It is visible all around us. In gardens and yards, flowers and plants are reaching toward the sun, offering both beauty and nutrition. In neighborhoods all around, those who are aware can observe the children who began June at one height, arrive in August's final days a few inches taller, some able to ride bikes without training wheels or swim the length of the pool. Those of us blessed to have college-aged young adults around are quite aware of the growth that has happened in the months that have passed. Summer makes that growing visible to family and friends and can be filled with both excitement and poignancy.

No matter the season—summer, fall, winter, spring—the longing for growth is a part of what it means to be human. We each, I believe, long to understand how our days, how our lives are adding up. And so it is always a good thing to ask the question: Did today find me merely coping? Or were there moments, true moments, when something nudged me to "moreness," toward some place of growth? Did I take the training wheels off something today or swim farther than ever before? Did I grow a few inches in understanding, in compassion, in peacefulness, in love? Was I able to reflect on the past nine months and see movement, perhaps, toward a hoped-for goal?

Over the past few days I have been traveling, and I intentionally left Thursday's horoscope in the pocket of an airplane seat for some unsuspecting traveler. If it was not found and discarded by a tenacious cleaning person, this question of growing or coping may now be rolling around in someone else's mind. It is a delicious thought. In the heat that has wrapped us all this summer, may we find only tiny moments of coping and instead find a reason to celebrate all that has grown.

Practice

Make a short list of ways in which you hope to grow. Commit it to memory. Create actions steps. Pray over this list. Place it in a visible place where you will see it each and every day.

Good Use of Time

Since returning from my vacation, I have been wading through all the things that can stack up over a week's time. Emails. Phone calls. Things you forgot to do before you left. Meetings. Laundry. You get the picture. So, I haven't made it to this space in my regular fashion. The time just seemed to get away from me.

Now that I have taken care of most of those things, I want to pass on something I observed today. I was driving down the very busy Hennepin Avenue to meet a friend for a long-planned birthday lunch. Half listening to the radio, I was reveling in the absolute beauty of this summer day. The cooler temperatures have moved in, making the sunny skies, the green of the grass and trees and colors of flowers even more brilliant than ever. It was one of those days when I actually thought to remind myself: "It is good to be alive." Very good.

Apparently I was not the only person who thought this. As I stopped at the stoplight on Hennepin and Franklin, I noticed the black car in the left-hand lane facing me. This car, headed north on Hennepin, had its blinker on to turn left at this busy intersection, always a tricky maneuver. The driver's car door was open and the driver was standing on the median waiting for the light to turn green. The driving was dancing! Right there for all the world to see! I watched as he grooved to the left and then the right. He snapped his fingers and twirled around. Michael Jackson-like. He jived first one way and then the other. He had the wonderful ability some people do of being able to swivel his head and neck in an amazing circular fashion. I could just faintly hear the beat he was hearing from his radio as it wafted across the airwaves toward my car. Its rhythm made my talk radio seem pretty dull.

Some people were crossing the street and chose to look down, trying to ignore this flight of fancy dancing. The woman whose car idled by mine furrowed her brow as she continued to talk on her phone. I wondered how they could not be taken in by this man, moved to dance, as he passed the time waiting for the light to change. He was a good dancer. He was enjoying himself. He was providing all of us with something "you won't see every day," as the saying goes. Why not drink it in, in all its fullness?

This dancing man was, after all, just making good use of what can feel like idle time. Sitting at a stoplight. Waiting to move from red to green. I have a friend who keeps a book on the front seat and reads at stoplights. While reading this might be safer, it certainly doesn't seem as much fun as dancing.

Watching him, I thought of that quote attributed to William W. Purkey. It urges us to stay in tune with the zest for life:

> *You've gotta dance like there's nobody watching,*
> *Love like you'll never be hurt,*
> *Sing like there's nobody listening,*
> *And live like it's heaven on earth.*

On this particular August day, with the sun shining down and traffic whizzing by, I was thankful for someone who had the courage to jump out of his car and dance. It was a good use of his time and a little reminder of another heavenly day.

Practice

Turn on some music. Dance! If this is too much of a stretch for you, listen to the music and imagine what you'd look like as a really, really good dancer. Now. . . . give it a try!

Close Encounters

A sacred being cannot be anticipated; it must be encountered. – W.H. AUDEN

We have had a strange winter visitor in our backyard. Last week my husband called me to the sliding glass doors that leads to our deck. Standing there looking back at me was an opossum. The creature stood just feet away, acting dazed and confused. For some reason instead of being repelled by this less-than-beautiful being, my heart broke.

Why was a nocturnal, hibernating animal walking around in broad daylight on a winter's day? All afternoon we followed its progress from deck to snowy yard. Once on the frozen ground under our black walnut tree, it ate the left-over bird seed that had been knocked to the ground. Two of the neighborhood children and I watched as it climbed a tree, resting in the branches for some time, tired from either lack of sleep or too much. The only reason we could come up with for its presence was the warmer temperatures we have experienced. It may have somehow been awakened prematurely. Its stunned and slow movements could have pointed to its being ill but I wanted to go with the warmer weather theory. The idea of having a sick, perhaps rabid, wild animal so close was a thought I did not want to entertain.

My heartbreak over this creature is that it brought to my consciousness all the other beings who find themselves misplaced, in the wrong place at the wrong time. Immigrants, wanderers made homeless by war, disaster, or a spiral of bad luck events like those we witness on the nightly news, those we read about in the morning newspaper. The opossum's eyes had that same dazed and confused look seen in those of people I pass on the street holding signs that read: "Mother needs money to buy milk" or "Veteran, please help." People displaced, confused, lost most often through no fault of their own.

This opossum no doubt lives under our deck and may have been there for longer than we know. And yet I had never encountered it before. It had been a silent part of our lives, and yet I could not have anticipated how this wild creature helped me see once again the sacred nature of all Creation. Its eyes met mine, and my heart was filled with compassion. Through this unexpected encounter I was reminded that the One who moves in the deepest winters and the abundance of spring cares for the least, the lost, and the lonely. I am grateful for the reminder.

Practice

Offer a prayer today for all those who are displaced, for all those who find themselves in places unfamiliar or frightening. Send words and energy of comfort and hope their way.

New Year's Practice

May the accolade for the first instant of the millennium (new year) make us aware
of its flip side: its precious emptiness. — JOSE REISSIG

I have never been one for resolutions at the New Year. There is something about them that brings out the rebellious side of me. I can quickly fall into the path of trying to outsmart myself with cheating my good intentions. Sound familiar? My mother might call this behavior the "bites off my nose to spite my face"syndrome, a common saying of hers. Of course, I am the only one to really suffer the failure of my own noble, though often ill-fated, attempts to better myself.

And so as we enter this New Year I have no grand illusions that I will create the ever-common list of resolutions: lose weight, exercise more, save more money . . . etc. . . . etc. Today's newspaper listed these among the top ten resolutions of most people. Though all these would be beneficial to me, this is not the road for me.

Instead I am thinking of my brothers and sisters in the faith who have learned from those who live in religious community. These are folks who take on what they refer to as a "practice." I like this word much better than discipline, another word that brings out my rebellious nature. To begin a practice, spiritual or otherwise, in the new year seems quite appealing. It also seems as if it might be a path to greater success.

According to definition, to practice is: *"To do repeatedly in order to learn or become proficient, to create a habit."* With this clean slate of a new year, I want to practice being healthier. Healthier and kinder. Kinder and more forgiving. More forgiving and fully present to each person I meet. My hope is to practice and practice. To learn, to become proficient at embracing what makes for a healthier mind, body, spirit.

Many of us practice doing things in which we will never be fully proficient. We play scales on a musical instrument without ever making it to the concert stage. We practice dance steps over and over knowing we will never "dance with the stars." Every day people practice a sport in which they will never be a standout. But there is such great joy in the practice. Tiny moments of beautiful music happen. The mastery of a turn or quick step raises heartbeats and confidence. And the physical engagement in those beloved sports build strength and sometimes a fun-filled community.

Practice. What practice is calling you in the emptiness of this year change? On the blank pages of this new year, what longing within you is waiting to be practiced until deep lessons are planted in your cells? Whatever is tugging at your heart on this final day of this year, may the new day and the new year find you stepping out with confidence to begin your practice. May each step be repeated over and over and over. Though we may not reach full proficiency, perhaps we will all feel as if we have learned much and are better people for it come year's end.

Practice

Today is the day. What is it you would like to practice? Ready, set, begin.

Longing

Tell it as a story
about darkness
giving birth to
light. . . . – JAN L. RICHARDSON

And so the winter days are unfolding. Here in Minnesota these days have been held under an even greater blanket of snow than usual, and the weekend promises even more. Cold temperatures which seem more like February are already filling our bones and causing people to walk around in the shoulders-to-ear, guarded fashion, eyes straight ahead looking ever toward the goal of the next warm place.

For those of us who are trying to pay attention to the season of Advent, the cold and snow provide the perfect backdrop to the play in which we are actors. This landscape spells longing, and longing is really one of the major feelings of Advent. Longing for what is unseen. Longing for what might be born in us. Longing to be awakened to the goodness and kindness the world often hides. Longing . . . so much longing.

If we allow the commercial world of Christmas sales to guide these days, we miss, I believe, such an important part of the process of this life's journey. To come face-to-face with the longings in our lives is an important task, a task that should not be left to the realm of regret. And so an Advent practice of reflection on our longings can bring us to a deeper understanding of what it means to be a person of faith, any faith really, not just the one that captures these December days.

Someplace in the darkness of our inner life something lurks. Not something frightening or evil, but something for which we long sometimes even beyond our knowing. For some it is meaning, for others a sense of peace. For some it is being loved, for others it is a place and experience of being known. Being known for who we really are not just what we do or what we own. For others it is a sense of hope that all will be well, in their lives and the lives of those they love.

This longing is multiplied by the fact that we are beings held together through community, through national and international connections. We long for the understanding and cooperation that would put an end to war. We long for the recognition of greed that harms the innocent. We long for the honoring of our blessed Earth home.

What longings are pulling at your heartstrings? What tugs at your soul in a way that will not let you go? On these days, in the middle of this season of waiting and watching, may the One who travels ever near hear your often silent voice and affirm your path.

Practice

Find a comfortable, cherished spot to spend some time in reflection. Notice the longings of your spirit. Breathe deeply the gifts of these longings.

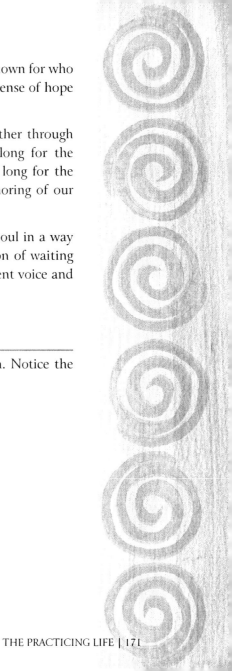

Shouting Stones

Some of the Pharisees in the crowd said to him,"Teacher, order your disciples to stop." He answered, "I tell you, if these were silent, the stones would shout out."
— LUKE 19:39-40

In Christian churches around the world, this Sunday is Palm Sunday, the last Sunday of Lent and the one before the celebration of Easter. It marks Jesus' entry into Jerusalem and the spiraling events that we have come to call Holy Week. In most churches it is a fairly joyous Sunday. There are processions of palm fronds being waved by children and more upbeat hymns than the minor-keyed ones of the Lenten season. At our church we often find it is a Sunday with higher attendance as families bring children to be part of this palm waving procession. Personally, I am never sure if it is the palm waving that brings people or the ever-increasing temperatures outside that simply make it easier to get small children up and out the door at an early hour. Whatever the cause, it makes for a rich and joyous Sunday.

The scripture that will be read is always the same story: Jesus friends are told to go find a donkey that has never been ridden before and tell the owner that their teacher needs it. For some reason, in the scriptures, there is not an argument with the owner; he just hands it over. Then Jesus begins this journey into Jerusalem where his ministry becomes very public, very quickly. As he becomes a part of a parade in which he is recognized as the one who has done miracles, who has healed the sick and welcomed the marginalized, excitement (and trouble) brews. The Pharisees warn the disciples to keep it down, to curb their enthusiasm. And then comes one of my favorite, somewhat obscure statements attributed to Jesus: *"I tell you, if these were silent, the stones would shout out."*

Shouting stones. The idea gives a person pause, doesn't it? I love the idea that if the human ones kept quiet about the movement of God in their lives, the stones would use their voices to speak. What might the voice of a stone sound like? To be honest, I think I've actually heard them. When I walk the beaches of the North Shore of Lake Superior, there are times when those flat black stones seem to speak to me of the awe and wonder of the magnificence around me. If I am too busy or too tightly wound with the stresses of my small life to notice, those stones will click together under my feet saying, "Wake up! Look around you! You are not the center of the universe!"

I would venture a guess that there are places in the world where the stones are shouting out their pain at the ways of war, of human greed and wanton killing. I would also bet there are places where the stones are speaking gentleness to soothe the tears of those who are lost in some personal wilderness, much like the heated stones my massage therapist uses to calm the tense muscles in my back. And then there are the stones piled into cairns, small monuments stacked with care by human hands, to mark places where a holy moment has happened and the human voice has no words to name the sacredness. These little altars can be found along highways, walking paths, and on mountain tops. Those stones continue to speak to a time of holiness not gone unnoticed.

This scripture also speaks to me of an earthy, earthly Jesus connected to the soil and place where he found himself living a full and complicated life. Grounded in the dusty, dirty roads of the small radius of country where he lived out his short, yet profound life, he loved the people and trusted the One who had breathed all of Creation into being. The people, the fig trees, the wells of water, the rivers of baptism, the mountains, the deserts, even the stones. All these had, indeed have, the gift of speaking truth to power if we have the ears to hear.

Practice

Today might be a good day to spend some time listening, really listening, to the rich voices that make up the day. What gifts are these voices offering you?

Reminder

Sometimes you simply need to hear your mother's voice in your head. And if your mother's voice is one that brings more turmoil than anything else, there are other voices that send gentle reminders. Today, for me, the reminder voice came from the daily newspaper's horoscope column: "Give yourself instruction and then follow it. Your directives don't have to be difficult. Ask yourself to do specific, simple tasks. The point is to put your higher self back in charge." Geminis who read this daily missive might have read the same thing.

Though I rarely skip a day's reading, this column does not always speak to me. But today's words cut to the quick. I have a million little loose ends floating around my head that simply need to be dealt with. Sound familiar? So I am setting about this morning creating the lists that will help clear out the clutter that has kept me from the more creative acts I want to pursue. Sewing up those dangling tasks will be the easy part of the horoscope to follow. But by clearing that path out, I will get to the important point: "putting my higher self back in charge."

I don't know about you, but I so often let the knit-picky, finger-pointing, shallow self be in charge of my daily actions. I get drawn into this little contention or that little piece of gossip and before I know it my day is consumed. Given the direction of my "higher self," I walk away from those little opportunities to gaggle around the water cooler, sharing useless, even harmful bits of news. Given the guidance of my higher self, I look for the good in every situation, the possibility rather than the limitation. Give the guidance of my higher self, I listen to the voice of Spirit to move me, to help me choose my words, to place before me the greater good in any given situation. This higher self is my Spirit-guided self. This is the self that is made in the image of God.

What instructions are you giving yourself today? What do you want to follow? Where is your higher self living these days? In the driver's seat, the back seat, or the trunk? Though this horoscope was meant for spring birthdays, I think those born in all seasons could benefit from its direction, don't you? If you are inclined, I invite you to share in this wise nugget to shape the day. We can all wait to see the surprises that "putting our higher selves in charge" might bring.

> *Lead a life worthy of the calling to which you have been called, with all humility and gentleness, with patience, bearing with one another in love, making every effort to maintain the unity of Spirit in the bond of peace.* — EPHESIANS 4:1

Practice

Allow your higher self to guide you this day. Take a moment and compose the horoscope you might follow to walk in the way of Spirit.

Wisdom and Peace

And have you brought the wisdom
That we have near lost?
Or have you brought the peace
That we're all aching for? – MARY McLAUGHLIN

Wisdom? Peace? These are words we often throw around with abandon particularly in church circles. We are "searching" for wisdom, we say as we look for the right answer to a question, a problem situation. We are trying to "find" peace as if it is a misplaced glove or a stray quarter. Wisdom and peace are two of the really big words that represent some of our core desires as humans. And yet they always seem just outside our reach. Why is that?

When I saw these words of Mary McLaughlin, I wondered what she meant in writing them. I had seen them in a book over Christmas break and jotted them down for further reflection. I did not know who Mary was so, in typical twenty-first-century fashion, I googled her. Of course, there were at least three people with that name who bubbled to the top of my Google search: a Celtic singer, a U.S. judge, and a ceramic box artist. Not knowing which Mary wrote the words made me wonder what each one might mean when they spoke the words "wisdom" and "peace." What might each have intended in writing this quote that caught my eye?

But, perhaps, that is not the point. The writer, whether singer, artist, or judge, looks outward toward someone who will bring whatever wisdom and peace is needed. And haven't we all done this? Looked to another person to bring the wisdom which will turn us toward vision, the compassion that will turn us toward peace. Rather than mining our own wisdom we look to someone else . . . perhaps someone older, richer, seemingly more powerful. Rather than listening for the deep peace that resides within, we wait for another to bring the olive branch.

We each carry the wisdom of our lives to offer the world. We each bring a small offering that can ignite a larger flame of peace. The mirror is ours to hold. And perhaps the time is now.

Practice

Set aside some time to be quiet and reflect on the places in your life that cry out for wisdom. Breathe deeply and allow the peace of breath to fill you fully. How might wisdom and peace be connected?

Search Potholes

There is an interesting and somewhat dangerous experience that happens in the waning days of winter. In places where the pavement of the road contracts and is often pummeled with salt and other chemicals, large potholes grow at an alarming rate. We have now entered such a time. Most streets, having frozen and thawed many times over the last months, are now filled with gaping holes, some as large as several feet in diameter. Many streets are so laden with these potholes that one must drive at reduced speeds, swerving and swaying to avoid destroying the car or disappearing into the hole altogether.

On my way into the office this morning I heard on the radio of a link on Minnesota Public Radio simply called "Search Potholes." It allows people to report potholes on various stretches of road. An area map is then marked with an orange flag to show the egregious pothole. Supposedly drivers might steer clear of these hazards by knowing where they are located. Visiting the sight, I saw that, at least in certain parts of the Cities it would be nearly impossible to drive any place!

"Search Potholes" got me thinking about these road nuisances in a more metaphorical way. I thought about the people I know who are experiencing some dangerous roads. Most of them did not know the "potholes" that steered their life in a different way, or brought it to a halt altogether, were out there. They were simply going along in their usual way when—"BOOM"—they hit a deep hole, breaking their speed and their spirit. I am thinking of a woman I know who is doing mighty battle for a second time with cancer. She had no idea the potholes were ahead of her, ready to zap her of her energy, her zest for living. I also think of those I know who are finding themselves out of work or under-employed, people who were just cruising along in their usual way and a big hole opened up in front them, threatening to swallow all they had known. Or then there are the people around the world whose lives have been turned upside down by the aftermath of a variety of devastating storms. As they literally pull themselves out of the mire, there must be so many days when they long to have had a sign, a warning of what was ahead. So many potholes.

Wouldn't it be wonderful if there was a way to search for the potholes that bring these kinds of stress and strain, even disaster, to our lives? Wouldn't it be wonderful to be able to go to a "Search Potholes" link and know which roads to avoid, which ones to take? Of course, there isn't. But there is wisdom to be gleaned from these pothole days. When you drive along a road with little knowledge of what it ahead, going a little slower helps. It also is wise to drive with intention, watching with wide eyes and an alert mind to the next pothole that might appear. It is also good to keep open and flexible, taking a turn that might result in a less bumpy ride. And it is really good to be gentle with yourself, snuggling deep into the padding of your car seat, finding a nice comfortable spot to protect you against the jar and jumble of the road.

The good news is that soon, when the days get warmer and the sun is higher in the sky, those potholes will get filled in, patched over, creating a smooth ride again. Sometimes it just takes a little waiting, a lot of patience and a good dose of prayer for those bumps in life to smooth out. And when that happens, we might realize that the potholes had lessons all their own.

Practice

Take a moment to remember the pothole places you have known. Is there a way to see the lessons they had to offer? Is there a way to feel grateful?

Empty

Today like every day we wake up empty
and frightened. Don't open the door to the study
and begin reading. Take down a musical instrument.
Let the beauty we love be what we do.
There are hundreds of ways to kneel and kiss the ground. – RUMI

Waking up empty. Did you wake up empty today? I am not talking necessarily about waking up with an empty stomach. It is probably a good sign when that happens. It means we did not eat so much yesterday that we are still full from a day of over-indulgence. That is not the emptiness I am talking about. We certainly know there are hundreds of thousands of people who wake up with empty stomachs, denied the life-giving nutrition most of us take for granted. May God's blessing be upon them today.

No, I am talking about a different kind of emptiness. That nagging feeling that makes a home at the center of who we are, longing to be filled with . . . what? Purpose? Creativity? Hope? Understanding? Companionship? God? This emptiness is that deep knowing that something is missing from our lives. It can be ignored temporarily but not forever. It can be anesthetized but not for long. This kind of longing left unattended breeds fear. Never a good thing.

We can try to fill this emptiness with all kinds of things—food, drink, overwork, distractions of all kinds. But in the end it is a longing that will not let us go because it somehow points us to a fuller knowledge of who we are, whose we are. I believe that in some way this emptiness, this longing to be filled, almost always points us toward some distance we experience from Spirit. The Sufi poet Rumi suggests that we find our way to filling this longing, not through more knowledge or greater study, but through allowing ourselves to do what we love. Sounds nice, doesn't it?

When was the last time you did something you truly love? Maybe you are one of those blessed people whose work allows them to do what they love every day. I feel that blessing in the work I do. But this "what we love" and its beauty takes many forms. What beauty is blessing your life, filling up the emptiness you feel? Is it time to tend this soil before it becomes a matter of urgency? Perhaps it already has.

As the earth is being washed of its winter dirt, preparing for the spring that will certainly come, it is a good time to reflect on what it is you truly love and all the beauty that produces. Allowing the rain to wash over whatever has accumulated, creating an emptiness, a longing waiting to be filled, it is an opportunity to connect once again to those things that fill us. Whether it is taking down an instrument to make music, or picking up a paint brush to paint, or reaching out to hold a child as you read them a story, or simply staring out the window into the middle distance, all these acts might be the one to bring beauty out of what you love. It would be a good thing to do not only for yourself but for the world. It would an act of gratitude.

It would be a prayer.

Practice

Take stock of your emptiness. Is it a good emptiness? What equal goodness would fill this empty place? Give yourself a gift of being filled today.

After Dark

Driving home from the office one evening this week, I witnessed a sight that made me laugh and filled me with curiosity. It was nearly dark, a little after 8:00 p.m. as I drove past a row of apartment buildings I pass with regularity. I always notice this block of apartments because there are often family groups sitting on the small porches, adults may be having conversations while children play close by with small toys. There is no play equipment near the apartments, no swing set or jungle gym. The children always seem to be entertaining themselves with whatever is at hand.

There is a stoplight at the corner by the apartments, and I had come to rest at the red light. That's when I noticed that the porches were empty, the lights now on inside the apartments, and the people, no doubt, tucked inside for the night. Except for one boy, probably about eight years old. He was crouching just off the porch in the shadows of a scraggly bush that has yet to find its summer foliage. I was intrigued. He looked around, as if to make sure he was alone, and began trying, over and over again, to do the deep knee bend dance movement most often associated with Russian dance, as seen in the soldier's dance in *Fiddler on the Roof.* The boy was determined. He jumped down, both knees bent as he tried to flick first one leg and then the other out at a right angle, his arms folded regally across his chest. My red light stop continued glowing as I watched him try over and over to execute this move. Just as the light went green, he did it. He successfully did the crouch-kick-crouch-kick move, and a huge smile spread across his face. And mine.

As I drove on I wondered what could have possibly caused this young boy to head outside on a warm spring evening to try this particular move. Had he seen someone else dance in this way? Was he too embarrassed to try it inside in front of family members no doubt trying to watch television or do homework? Maybe he was in a school play and this was a part of his big dance number. Who knows? But the sight gave me such joy.

I thought of all the times I have imagined myself creating a move I have seen someone else do that seemed beautiful, graceful. I wanted to be able to do that too. Why, even as recent as the Winter Olympics I tried to imagine myself doing some of the ice skating spins that the skaters were doing. When I mentioned this, my husband pointed out that knowing how to ice skate might be a first step! I think of some of the lovely movements I see people do on my guilty pleasure show, "Dancing With the Stars." Watching these brave people learn new steps each week and then show them off in front of an audience always gives me the itch to try also. I can imagine there are many people who, after watching the show, try a few of the steps in the privacy of their own homes. Lifting arms, gliding across the floor in sweatpants or sneakers, for at least a moment we can have the opportunity to do our own sweet moves.

Maybe that is what lured the young boy outside just as dark approached to see if he, too, could do "that move." The dream of being able to kick, spin, leap, and slide have kept people dancing throughout time. I am glad the dream and the tradition continue, aren't you? Tonight could be a fine one for dancing. I say, go for it!

Dancing is like dreaming with your feet! – CONSTANZE

𝒫ractice

Everyone has a bucket list of things they want to try to do. What is yours? Today is the day!

Horoscope

Taoist philosopher Lao Tzu said: "The journey of a thousand miles begins with one step." Right now, said journey feels more like 50 thousand miles. And still the work is the same: one step at a time.

What to do with a morning that begins with a horoscope like this? That is my day's quest. When I read this daily, sage advice, I laughed out loud. The blending of the wisdom of Buddhist teaching and the guidance of the stars tickled my funny bone. But within a few minutes it brought me to a deeper place. What journey am I on right now? In my life. In my work. This year. This day. What about your journey? Where is your journey taking you?

The metaphor of journey is so rich. I do think about it often, and yet I am not sure I truly live with the powerful gift of it. It is so easy to get up every morning and plan a day in which much may be "accomplished" but few miles are traveled. Days can be frittered away, checking off the little details that nag at any life. But what about the journey? Has the first step even been taken? Or in the accomplishments is the movement more stationary than forward?

This stepping out is so much easier to recognize in others than it is in oneself. It is so easy to look at someone else and ascertain whether or not you think they are making steps on their journey. I can give all kinds of opinions about choices people are, or are not, making that will move them on their path. It is not so easy, or comfortable, to always be as honest with myself. The excuses come much more quickly about what is keeping me from taking that important first step.

So, receiving this free, guiding advice via the morning paper has brought me up short, has thrown the mirror toward my own waiting face. Like most people, I have a few deep desires that fall into the "some day" category. "Some day" I'll finish that manuscript. "Some day" I'll lose those extra pounds. "Some day" I'll mend that wounded relationship. Some day . . . some day . . . some day. . . .

As always, I am happy to share my horoscope with anyone who thinks it fits their journey on this "one day at a time" life. It sure spoke to mine.

Practice

What are your "some days"? What journey is asking one step from you? Given the fragility of each precious day, perhaps today is the one on which to take the first, important step.

Tough

Be tough in the way a blade of grass is: rooted, willing to lean, and at peace with what is around it. – NATALIE GOLDBERG

Natalie Goldberg is a writer, poet, and teacher who practices Buddhism. Her books on writing have been an inspiration to me. Yesterday I came across this quote in another book while searching for prayers of healing to be spoken in worship this Sunday. I do not know in what context she originally wrote these words. But it caused me to think about what it means to be "tough." Sometimes our lives require us to be "tough" even when we find this an uncomfortable way to be, even when it goes against our nature. I think of the ways in which parenting calls us to offer tough love to children who cannot see the whole picture, who cannot understand the possible far-reaching implications of their actions. I think of leaders who, though full of compassion and empathy, find is necessary to be tough in a situation, to set clear boundaries for those they lead. I am reminded of the many times Moses needed to be tough with those he shepherded through the wilderness or how Jesus was clear with the disciples about the length to which they were to go to serve those around them. I think of our national leaders who find often find themselves in situations requiring a toughness that they never imagined.

Being tough is not, I believe, the same as being stubborn. Most of the time, when we are stubborn, we are mostly interested in being "right." Being stubborn does not allow us to be present to the fullness of a situation, does not allow us to have perspective on how our actions affect others or even how the actions of others affect us. Being stubborn is about holding our ground, defining our turf, and rarely holds much peace.

At the times when toughness is called for, it is important to remember who you are and to be content with that. I cannot utter a guess at what a blade of grass knows or doesn't know, but I can imagine each blade feels its rootedness in the soil and has some comfort with that. I can imagine that, just as a cool breeze on a summer's day feels good to my human skin, the breeze that blows the blade of grass has an effect on its connection to the other blades around it without taking away from its own "bladeness." As humans this is a good lesson to learn. In the midst of any tumult or trial, to hold onto one's sense of self without being overly influenced by the feelings, opinions and comments of the other "blades" around is the beginning of deep self-knowledge.

This deep self-knowledge can lead to a sense of peace about what is around—other blades of grass, decisions that are difficult, big life questions, transitions we didn't choose, illness that threatens. Being able to know how our roots reach down and yet being able to lean in the winds that will, no doubt, come our way can bring the peace of realizing that we are still standing. Some days, most days, that is simply enough.

Practice

Reflect on times when you have needed to be tough. What did you learn from such times? Affirm yourself for being as tough as you needed to be and for bending when it was necessary.

Stepping into the River

At this time, Jesus came from Nazareth in Galilee and was baptized by John in the Jordan. The moment he came out of the water, he saw the sky split open and God's Spirit, looking like a dove, come down on him. Along with the Spirit, a voice: "You are my Child, chosen and marked by my love, pride of my life."
— MARK 1: 9-11 (THE MESSAGE)

This past Sunday is what is know in the church year as Baptism of Jesus Sunday. It always feels a bit peculiar to me. We have just finished Christmas, celebrating the *birth* of Jesus. Some people have yet to put away all the manger scenes that dot their house. We skip right over the few verses that say anything about Jesus as a boy. Instead we jump right into the beginning his ministry, his way of showing God's Way in the world. For this, the scriptures tell us, he must be baptized by his cousin John. Wild, crazy John. And so he steps into the River Jordan, and nothing is ever the same again. He hears the voice of God echoing around him, speaking unconditional love and acceptance, and off he goes.

Not many people I know can remember their baptism. I certainly can't, though I have seen pictures. Pictures of a small baby made miniature by the flowing white dress that clothes her. She is held by a beautiful young woman standing by a smiling young man, whose faces speak of unconditional love and acceptance if not down right adoration. Certainly, at the time, my baptism was not the kind of life-changing experience that Jesus had. But it was the start of being marked over and over by the love of a faith community, and for that I am eternally grateful.

Everyone has experiences where they have stepped into a river and their life was forever changed. In our community on Sunday people told of just such moments. Being married and learning what it means to be a partner. Having children, and the joy and chaos that life shift brings. Admitting their powerlessness over alcohol.

Taking the first step of healing after a parent's death. Encountering the world through travel and feeling that connection in newfound ways. The stories were rich, and we could still be there hearing them all. They carried the fullness of life.

The experience caused me to think of all the "stepping into the river" experiences I have had. It also allowed me to remember these pivotal events that I have seen happen in our country and our world. Depending on one's age, these moments are different but they are the markers by which we gauge our lives. There are always the "pre" and "post" times. Like before the war, after September 11. Before the recession, after the election. Before graduation, after the baby was born. The moments go on and on. They are important markers, and they provide a certain balance that helps us map what it means to be human.

When have you stepped into the river and never been the same? Perhaps you are at just such a point right now. Whether remembered or about to be experienced, may you, may each of us, find in this moment an encounter with the Holy. An encounter in which we are bathed with the message: "You are my Child, chosen and marked by my love, pride of my life."

Blessed be.

Practice

Write down the pivotal moments when you "stepped into the river" and were changed. Was someone else a part of this experience? Offer a prayer for all the times you have had these kinds of encounters.

Paths

Recently I had the pleasure of observing the many miles of snow-covered land between the Twin Cities and Milwaukee. It is one of my favorite drives. I love looking out at the various farms, some looking modern with ranch-style, one-level houses, and others with the white, two-story structures with wraparound porches that seem to signal a by-gone day. The barns in their various colors—red, lots of red . . . green . . . brown . . . white . . . even blue—make colorful markings against the stark white of the rolling fields. In some places straw or stray cornstalks interrupt the snowy landscape, making their death-brown look much more beautiful than it really is. In just a few short months (we hope!) the rich soil will be teeming with seeds and growth. Corn and soybeans will once again create the picture of abundance out the car window. But for now there is white, shining brilliant and crusted from strong winds and powerful doses of sunshine.

After several miles of allowing my eyes to take in this wintry scene, I began to notice the places where paths had been cut in the snow. There were those places where snowmobiles zoom by at what seems tremendous speeds, cutting this way and that at the sides of the roads, often charging across the road like the deer we know to watch out in autumn. These paths were made for fun and a sense of freedom.

There were cross country ski paths that meandered through open fields and into the woods that ring the highway. The sight of those paths bring a feeling of calm and that whooshing sound that is only made by the sound of skis on snow. I imagined the skiers moving away from the frantic traffic of the highway into the depths of the woods where they stopped to catch their breath. Allowing the silence they now had found to wash over them, I thought of them drinking in the smell of the evergreens, the moist earth, the air that chilled their lungs. These were paths for connecting to the earth and to one's heartbeat.

Every now and then I would notice other paths made not by humans or their toys but by animals whose footprints were too far away for me to identify. One set of prints created this wonderful winding, circular pattern, in and out, around and back, as if they had been playing a child's chasing game. This path made me smile.

Then, of course, there were the paths made by the faithful, predictable cows as they headed from the field where they had been observing bovine life. At some signal known only to them, they turned from the spot where they had spent the morning or afternoon and headed toward the barn, to be milked and to be fed. Their path was one of habit and nurture.

Paths. We travel them everyday. Some we travel so often we no longer see the scenery we pass by. I have often driven for several blocks, perhaps even longer, and have no memory of having done so, the path is so familiar to me. Have you ever done this? It's rather sad in a way to think that those places we know best have nothing left to offer us in the way of surprise.

There are the paths we choose and those that become the detour we never expected or wanted. And yet, there the path is unfolding before us, and we have no choice but to take step after step after step until we make some sense of where it is taking us. I know several people right now who are trying to make sense of the detour that has become their path. May God bless them.

One of my favorite scriptures is from Jeremiah: *"Stand at the crossroads, and look, and ask for the ancient paths, where the good way lies; and walk in it, and find rest for your souls."* The fact of the matter is that sometimes the ancient paths, the good way, can seem quite elusive. Or it can seem as if we are walking a path that continues to turn and turn in ways that create anxiety and fear. Still other times, we can be paralyzed by not being able to choose which way to turn on the path that lies before us. Every now and then we are blessed with an understanding of our path that is so sure, so true, we walk confidently, with assurance, never looking back.

Wherever you are on the path this day, may you find some ancient wisdom that holds you, some goodness that unfolds before you, and some deep rest for your soul.

Practice

Notice the paths you travel. Are they ones you have chosen? Are they filled with wisdom? Today choose a new path and explore what it might have to offer you.

Let It Go

There are courageous, daring people who will go to great lengths to spread a message. Some of these messages come in the form of what some people would name graffiti, words painted on highway signs hung far above moving traffic. When I see these words suspended in mid-air, many in languages I do not speak, I try to imagine when these words were painted. How did the writer make their way to the precarious precipice with a spray paint can in hand? Was someone hanging onto them for dear life while they wrote their message for the world to see? How were they not seen, perhaps arrested? At what time of day or night did this happen without being spotted? Did they dangle upside down, held by their ankles by an accomplice, chosen to be the writer because they have the ability to form letters backwards or inverted?

One weekend in early April, I came upon one of these highway messages. This one did not take such acrobatics. Its message did not use paint but what appeared to be strips of cloth woven through a freeway overpass bridge made of chain link fence. Carefully threaded through the links of the hard metal, in neatly created third-grade cursive writing, were three simple words: "Let it go."

Let it go. Seeing these words made me smile, made my shoulders relax away from my ears, allowed me to take a little deeper breath. Let it go. I imagined all the people who have traveled and are traveling past this message even as I write this. People who need to have someone say these very words to them. People who are clutching the steering wheel too tightly. People who are clenching their jaw, grinding their teeth unknowingly as they hold onto—what? Fear? Dread? Anger? Hurt? Failure?

I know these people because, several times a day, I am one of them. In an effort to create a life, I can try to control so many things, things over which control is

only in illusion. And because that illusion becomes the focus of my attention, I can send messages to the muscles in my body to "Hold on." Hold on. I am going to conquer this. Hold on. I can make this come out just like I want it to. Hold on. Hold on. Hold on.

"We must let go of the life we have planned, so as to accept the one that is waiting for us," says Joseph Campbell. This is a difficult message for most of us. Yet so many of the world's faith traditions carries this very wisdom. The season of Lent has this letting go at its center. We read the sacred texts that tell of Jesus' eternal letting go into the living out of God's call in his life. His works of compassion, mercy, healing, and hope led to events over which he had no control. His life was a continual letting go into love. And so it is with each of us.

How does the message "let it go" sound in your life today? How do these words come into your eyes and ears and find a home? What needs "letting go"? What is really at stake in doing so?

Someplace in the two cities I love there lives a messenger who has less fabric than they did a week ago. They used those pieces of cloth to send a message to all who need it, to all who will listen, to all who will answer its call.

I am grateful.

Practice

As you create your "to do list" for this day, make room for a few things that need to be let go. Pay attention to how that feels in your body. Is it something that would be helpful to do every day?

Breathe on Me

In a recent newspaper article, I was interested in a writer's words debunking certain plant facts or fiction. I was particularly drawn to several paragraphs about talking to your plants. Now this is an idea that has been around for many years, and I have certainly observed many people speaking loving words to their plants. I haven't, however, done any hard research to see if talking while watering and weeding really makes any difference. I mostly have just thought it was sweet, a lovely thing to do between plant and gardener.

It seems, according to the writer, that it does indeed breed healthier plants. It does not really matter much what the love words you say are as long as you breathe long and hard on them. It seem the human's inhalation of oxygen and exhalation of carbon dioxide goes up against the plant's "exhalation" of oxygen and "inhalation" of carbon dioxide. As we are talking to these leafy ones, our breath feeds their need for CO_2. It's kind of a mouth to leaf thing.

Breathing is important business for people, plants and, well, all living things. But it is certainly something we take for granted. In fact, I know people who often hold their breath unconsciously when under stress. Breathing well regulates our hearts and calms our tensions. Breathing deeply lowers our blood pressure and can take us to a place of meditation. Paying attention to our breath can also help us connect to Spirit, allowing our prayers and our breath to unite. And it seems our breathing can also bring much needed greenness to the world.

On this winter day, it would be a good thing to spend some time breathing . . . just breathing . . . connecting with the Life Force that keeps us moving through this amazing and ever-changing world. Breathing in, we are filled with the Spirit. Breathing out, we exhale a life-giving form that causes plants to grow and flowers to bloom. Feels good, doesn't it?

Practice

Find a quiet spot and get comfortable, feet on the ground, eyes closed. Breathe naturally, noticing the rhythm of your own breathing. Simply be with your life-giving breath for a determined amount of time. Try to carry this practice into every day.

Available

Smile, breathe, go slowly. – THICH NHAT HAHN

This January I began fulfilling a long-time desire. I began practicing yoga. While I had taken a few classes here and there, it never seemed to stick. The time was wrong. I was too busy. Once the room was even too cold to make me stick with it! But this new endeavor seems to be turning out much better. I love the attention to breath—so important to so many things . . . stress reduction, anger management, prayer. And I love the music they play . . . mostly soothing and contemplative.

One of the words used quite often by the teacher is "available," as in "if this is available to you." She says this as she is moving into a particular pose, stretching her limber body in all manner of shapes. In this context "available" means "if you can do this." It is such a nice grace-filled way of approaching a pose that, many times, seems to me pretty impossible! But I never feel shamed or too old or unable; the pose simply isn't available to me yet. Which in turn implies that it will be some day. It is a very hopeful feeling. Plus each time the teacher says "available" it makes me smile, and that has to also be good for my practice, doesn't it? Smiling several times an hour, while breathing deeply and stretching my muscles into various lunges, has to be doing something wonderful in my body and my spirit.

There are many things in life that are not available to us on any given day. These unavailable acts are based on so many factors—experience, education, economics, where we were born, the list goes on and on. But just because they are unavailable today does not mean they will always be so. I know this from my very short practice of yoga so far. The first several times I tried Tree pose, it was more like tree-in-wild-storm pose. My body whipped this way and that, falling over every time. And then one day, after a few short weeks, I did it. I stood tall and still, not for very long, but I did it! Tree was available to me. I felt such a surge of energy and power.

Of course, the next day I tried to become my Tree the winds were blowing once again. But I am still holding onto the day when Tree pose and I became one. This small little piece of wisdom learned through yoga has filtered out into my understanding of other things in life that may be available . . . or not. Sometimes patience seems completely unavailable. Same with forgiveness. And compassion. That's where practice comes into play. The more I practice a patient mind, a forgiving heart, a compassionate spirit, they become slowly available.

And so that is one of the true lessons of this short yoga practice I have begun. The time set aside for connecting with this breath that keeps each of us moving on the earth sets in motion the notion that much becomes available to us when we practice and practice and practice.

What would you like to move from the unavailable to available spot in your life? What pose would you like to hold and strengthen until you are full of energy and power? May we all find the joy of this "available" to us and may our hearts be lifted in gratitude.

Practice

What would you like to move from the unavailable to the available spot in your life? What pose would you like to hold and strengthen until you are full of energy and power? There is no time like the present to begin your practice.

Tingling Fingertips

Our spirits would stretch out the way the light of the sun spreads through the sky. Our breaths came out, through our lungs, throats, soles, skin; we exhaled from our tingling fingertips. We breathed; we lived.

– TAN TWAN ENG, *The Gift of Rain*

I began this morning staring out at Lake Superior. As I quietly watched the sun's light come up on this powerful and beautiful body of water, I was struck with the ways in which the wind moved upon the water, creating patterns that moved both toward the shore and away. The dancing of this unseen force moved this mighty lake in ways over which it has no power. Under the water a similar force united with the force above to create the waves that dashed against the unmoving rocks. I could hear the sound of the crashing as it formed a rhythm not unlike the one beating in my own chest, rising with my breath.

That is when I realized I had a short chant we have often used in worship echoing in my head: "The wind blows where it will, you know not where it's coming from or where it's going to." This chant written by Trisha Watts carries a tune that resembles the flowing in and out of a wave. I allowed the music that came from my unconscious to flow over me, becoming a morning prayer.

The words of this chant, of course, come from the scriptures. It is an attempt to describe how the Spirit moves in and out of our lives and the life of all Creation. This breathing, this unseen yet powerful force, is like our breath. It is that which brings life. Even a life over which we have very little control. Even a life that can surprise and befuddle us. Even a life that can become chaos and filled with tumultuous questions.

Many cultures honor what we refer to as the four elements: earth, water, fire, air. The first three are visible to us—in some ways, easy to grasp. But air—breath,

spirit—can only be known by its effect. As I continue to look out the window at this enormous body of water, I see the trees and water animated by the unseen force of wind. Just a few miles north, the fires that are moving through the beloved forests of the Boundary Waters are fueled by the air that fans the flames. Flames that will not only destroy but will also eventually bring new life to the earth through seeds that are scattered and soil that is renewed.

What to make of all this? For me, it is that unseen power of Spirit that is always present. In the Hebrew scriptures the word *ruach* is one and the same for Spirit, breath, wind, and air. It is the same word used to describe the Holy's moving across the initial waters bringing life, in all the forms known to us, out of the teeming waters of chaos. Unseen yet life-producing.

An encounter with the waters of Lake Superior never ceases to restore confidence in me. Its sheer presence reminds me of the largesse of the world of which I am only a tiny part. Somehow this makes any problem or distress I may be experiencing seem manageable. It is, in that sense, a grounding presence, I guess. And the wind that moves, always moves, over its surface and under its waves grounds me in the reassurance of the Spirit's presence moving in my life. In ways I understand and that are visible. In ways that are unseen and surprising.

And yet always in ways that lead to life . . . all the way to our tingling fingertips.

Practice

Turn the palms of your hands upward and allow them to rest in your lap. Notice all the lines and patterns that make your hands unique. While looking at your hands, imagine all that is unseen that brings you life. Imagine these invisible forces to rest in your outstretched hands. Say a prayer for all you hold.

Vigilant

These are days that call us to be vigilant. I am not talking about any particular political or social vigilance. Nor am I speaking of a vigilance toward justice or even compassion. Though all these forms of living a vigilant life are important and needed, I am not speaking about the kind of passion about an issue or situation that pulls us into that focused, often single-mindedness I often think of as vigilance.

Instead, I am speaking about a vigilance that keeps us awake to the ways the world is being transformed around us. Those of us blessed to live where the pattern of seasons brings a colorful landscape to autumn know that in the blink of an eye, or movement of strong wind, the beauty of reds, oranges, and yellows that are now dotting our yards and parks can disappear. It is important to be awake and aware so as not to miss a moment of the passage, this visible metaphor of the rhythms of life.

I have tried to remember this as I have been driving about the Twin Cities this week. On the North Shore of Lake Superior last weekend, the colors were just beginning to show themselves. The birches were screaming their brassy yellow song as they stood nestled in the stable evergreens. One needed to go off the beaten path to see any sight of the red of maples dwarfed by these taller trees who love the colder climates. But the color is emerging with each passing hour throughout the city. It can be a full-time job to watch it all happening!

This year I have been aware of the numbers of trees that have shown their colors in a distinctive way. Instead of an "all over" showing of their autumn colors, these trees that have caught my attention remain green on one side or section while another part is showing ruby, gold, and topaz colors. The contrasts of a tree dressed is such segmented colors stops me in my tracks. Maybe it has always been this way and I have just not noticed.

It brought to mind a report I heard the other evening that once again explained the process by which trees "change" their color. The point was made that trees don't really change color. They have the colors we see in autumn already in their leaves. The reds and yellows and oranges have been there all along and just emerge with the changes in sunlight, temperatures, and climate.

This idea, this truth of nature, made me smile. It did so because the same is true of each of us, isn't it? I have always been stunned by the idea that each of us is born with a uniqueness that travels with us throughout our lives. Sometimes parts of us, buried deep within rise to the surface and we are seen, and see ourselves, in new ways. We carry all these gifts that need the right light, soil, environment to be given the power to emerge at a time that is often beyond our control or even awareness. Like the leaves that carry these rich colors that startle and amaze us in autumn, we also carry surprises we have yet to discover. This very idea makes me feel so hopeful.

I love knowing that there is within each of us a deep red of passion and its sister, compassion, waiting to emerge when the need and light are right. It calms me to know that there is a warm, yellow swath of courage flowing just under the skin. When it no longer seems possible to hold forth in a green, growing way, it brings me peace to know that a glow of orange will carry each of us to a place of rest. All these colors, and so many others, have been with us all along. Just as it is with the trees who now are making their own transformations in their own sweet time.

May we each have the patience and wisdom and vigilance to embrace what lies at our depths and to give to the world the beauty we posses.

Practice

Spend time today reflecting on what colors are untapped in you. What gifts Re you withholding from yourself and the world. Make a commitment to those deeply planted parts of yourself waiting to be awakened.

Remembering Iona

One year ago today, I was full of excitement. I was about to embark on a much-planned and much-anticipated pilgrimage to Scotland and particularly the tiny island of Iona. My bags were packed, and my walking stick was nestled among warm layers of waterproof clothing. I had spent the previous months in conversation and worship with the others who also would make the journey. I remember spending this final day before leaving tending to the little details one needs to accomplish before any effort to leave home and work for awhile. By day's end, the list I had made was all crossed off.

Today I have been thinking about the pilgrimage itself and the year that has passed. I have been reflecting on the fact that, I believe, not one day has gone by when I did not think of my time on Iona at least once during the day. I will be in traffic, and a thought will fly across the movie screen of my brain reminding me of the beauty of green, rolling hills covered with the burnt-orange of bracken. Sitting in meetings that may last too long or are filled with agendas that do not feed my spirit, I will once again imagine myself sitting in the pews of the ancient stone cathedral where ferns could be seen growing randomly out of the moist, cold walls. Yesterday, as the winds blew around my car on the freeway, I felt my tin-can container move slowly side to side and thought of the night on the island when the wind made such a whooshing circle around the abbey that the Presence of the Holy Spirit was known by each of us who worshiped together. The smallest thing can connect me with the gifts of this time of intentionality looking for God's presence in a place known to be sacred to so many for so many years.

What makes a place sacred? What makes our experience of a place sacred? I have pondered this question many times over the last year. Each of us on the pilgrimage brought our expectations and hopes, all of them different. We each had

our motivations for making this trip, for setting aside the time and resources to be on a walk together in a land that was foreign to us, in pursuit of an encounter with the Holy. Perhaps an element of the sacred nature of any place are the expectations we bring.

But I do believe there are places where the very ground, the air, the people and beings create a container in which others experience the movement of the Holy in specific ways. On Iona, perhaps the sacred ground is tilled by the hundreds of thousands of prayers that have been said on this tiny piece of earth. Prayers of joy, sorrow, grief, hope, water the soil. Certainly the prayers of expectation each pilgrim carries as they step from the ferry nurtures the garden that will become that person's experience of the One we call God and plant seeds for those who will come after.

I know that, for me, my experience of the Holy was made manifest by those whose work it was to welcome. Volunteers and residents of the island clearly understand their life's work is to welcome the pilgrims who arrive daily, weekly, monthly, yearly, as the waters of the sea that surrounds allows. As we were welcomed and sent on our way by those we had only met, I knew that God was in that place. It was holy ground.

And so tomorrow, I will once again remember the gift that last year's pilgrimage was and how it travels with me still. I will remember and give thanks. For sacred places and for those who welcome.

> *Then Jacob woke from his sleep and said, "Surely the Lord is in this place—and I did not know it!"*
>
> – GENESIS 28:16

Practice

In a time of quiet, think about the places that are sacred to you. Allow the names of those places to come to your mind and speak those names aloud. These sacred places can form a mantel of protection and awe for you. Wear it well.

Bridge Closed Ahead

Breath is the bridge which connects life to consciousness, which unites your body to your thoughts. – THICH NHAT HAHN

There is a saying in Minnesota that there are really only two seasons: winter and road construction. We are firmly planted in the later in these waning August days. Everywhere we travel there is the prevalence of bright orange—cones, signs, trucks, and equipment. Sprinkled throughout this sea of orange are all the many workers in their brilliant yellow-green vests. It can make for a very colorful drive as we weave in and out of roads that have been diverted or routes that have been changed. One of the things I like about this time of year is that driving demands a certain caution and an awareness of, not only the other drivers, but of all those precious human bodies working on our behalf as cars speed by them.

For some reason this past week I have become very aware of one particular sign as I make my way on my familiar route between church and home, home and church. Among all the other bright orange messages, one stands out: Bridge Closed Ahead. Perhaps I am aware of it because it is impossible to see without thinking of the many bridges I cross each day on this simple journey. The ways in which the Mississippi River snakes through the Twin Cities makes it nearly impossible not to cross a bridge at one point or another. Bridges make our living here possible.

But bridges are also such a wonderful metaphor. We need these connectors not only in a literal sense but also in our relationships, our creative lives, our understanding of faith, the living of our unfolding days. How many times I have needed just the right words that will bridge a hurt I have caused another. How many times I have searched for and finally found the perfect bridge that connected an idea I had been birthing to another person's idea, creating an answer to a problem, a fuller picture of how to move forward. How many times I have heard one person's words about God's movement in their lives, words that have built a bridge to a greater understanding of God's movement in my own. And how often I am in the presence of someone of another generation and experience the building of a bridge of years that brings me greater insight and generosity with where I am in my own life.

Bridges are important. They connect us and help us move from one place to the next. But I am also aware of people who are up against a "bridge closed ahead" sign and do not know how to re-route themselves. No detour is in sight or seems possible. That message of the bridge that is unavailable can be a devastating experience. I've experienced it, have you?

Perhaps I am also aware of bridges because I have just returned from a road trip where many bridges were crossed. Bridges across rivers and streams and through the Low Country waters of South Carolina. As we made our way across bridge after bridge, nothing had prepared us for the most magnificent bridge of all: the Talmadge Bridge that led us into the beautiful city of Savannah. It is a bridge that actually bows up in the middle and at one point you cannot see the other side. It feels as if you might be driving off into the water of the horizon. It makes your stomach leave you.

What bridges are you crossing these days? What bridges have closed for you? Which bridges seem to be sending you into the abyss? Each day is a bridge between this day's gift of life and the next. May each of us be led gently from one side to the other. May we have faithful companions for the journey. May we have the courage and the patience to re-route ourselves when a bridge closes. And may the One who breathed us into being be beside us at every turn.

Practice

Imagine all the bridges that have been a part of your journey so far. Where did they lead you? Pay attention today to the places where bridging happens. Commit yourself to being a bridge for others.

Contentment

The wonderful thing about simplicity is its ability to give us contentment. Do you understand what a freedom this is? To live in contentment means we can opt out of the status race and the maddening pace that is its necessary partner. We can shout "NO!" to the insanity which chants, "More, more, more!" We can rest contented in the gracious provision of God.

– RICHARD FOSTER, *Freedom of Simplicity*

Every morning I receive an email with a short piece of prose or poetry from a website called "Inward/Outward." These writings never fail to nudge me and fill my spirit. Today's offering was no exception. These words by Richard Foster hit me with their full power.

Contentment. Now, there is a word we don't hear often or, at least, not often enough. Its pursuit seems, in so many ways, counter-cultural, at least in our North American way of seeing the world. To be contented must mean we are not working hard enough, our goals are not high enough, our desires not full enough. We are taught from a very early age to "never be contented" with what we have but to strive for more . . . whatever more means. It is the way we reach beyond ourselves toward a success that is planned just for us by some unseen force we cannot name. This is the message that sometimes gets labeled "The American Dream."

Now I don't want to give the idea that I have anything against the creation and pursuit of goals, of making a good life. To create a comfortable, safe, productive life in which we pursue what we love doing, are surrounded by people we love, in which we have our basic needs met, is what I believe we mean when we talk about the "common good" for all. It is a way of life that understands that "more" is not necessarily better. Understanding the simplicity of "enough" in our lives can lead to this experience of contentment.

Perhaps I was drawn to these words because for whatever reason I had a full body experience of contentment this past weekend. It was not a particularly profound experience but one I did take note of. My weekend was simple, not too many things going on. I did a little work around the house, replanted some flowers in a window box, took a trip to the farmer's market, and then sought relief from the heat inside the house. At one point of the afternoon I walked to a neighborhood coffee shop and did a little writing and spent time with a novel. At one point of this experience I realized that my body had relaxed into the soft leather, low-slung chair. I looked around at the other people present. One man was nursing a cup of coffee while playing solitaire on his computer. A woman and her young daughter were having a sweet, intimate conversation, their heads close to one another as they shared this time on a sweltering Saturday afternoon. Another couple, a man and woman, were engaged in a quiet conversation; I heard bits and pieces that showed their genuine concern for one another. The ceiling fans whirred overhead as my iced coffee glass produced moisture on its surface. I nestled even further into this comfy chair, recognizing the pure contentment I felt.

All was not completely right with the world or our country or even our state. All was not even completely right in my own life. But I was still contented. Contented to have what I needed, to be able to read a good book and have a cool drink to ward off the heat. Contented to have enough provisions that I recognized God's movement in it all. My prayer is that, each day, all people may have a glimpse of just such contentment. Enough of a glimpse to embrace a simplicity that leads to a life of contentment and freedom for all . . . one day at a time, one life at a time.

Blessed be.

Practice

Make a list of all the ways in which you experience contentment. If you cannot find anything on your list, begin to count the blessings in your life. Perhaps contentment rests someplace within these blessings.

Thank-able

This past week I received a letter from Douglas Wood, the author of such wonderful books as *Old Turtle* and *Granddad's Prayers of the Earth*. I have been a fan for some time and we have invited him to be our guest at Hennepin Church this year. He was confirming with me the details of the day and sending along a contract. Tucked inside the envelope was also a bookmark-sized paper that had a list of suggestions on "How to be a Writer." As I read the list I was filled with laughter, with a sense of hope and even a glint of tears.

I have read this list over and over in the last few days. I shared it as a devotional with our staff on Tuesday. The list includes things like: Wake up . . . Attend sunrises . . . Skinny dip . . . Pack light . . . Learn to stop stepping on rakes . . . Notice how unusual everything is . . . Do the thing you fear . . . and on and on. At one point I actually decided I would adopt one thing per day to focus on and see where it might take me.

Of course, I do want to be a writer so I welcome every "how-to" successful folks like Wood can offer. But mostly I realized these suggestions were equally as helpful in how to just be a good human being, a good "I love this life" kind of human being. Which is what, if I am honest, is what I want to be most of all.

So on Tuesday I took up this suggestion: "Know that The News is not the world." This one came in quite handy given the crazy-making news coming at us fast and furious from any number of media sources. Listening to the reports of greed and corruption, I reminded myself of the gentle, gracious, fun-loving people I have met in my life. I thought of the waves of God's Presence that have washed over me as I have walked the emerald green countryside and rocky beaches. I remembered the healing power of caring and groves of trees that connected me with ancient wisdom that transcends the momentary flourish of powerful people behaving badly. This is the world. I felt blessed to be reminded.

Tomorrow I plan to take up another point on the list: "Thank everything that's thank-able." I have been thinking about it all afternoon, planning my strategy. And here is the rub: What isn't thank-able? When I wake up in the morning, a thanks goes to the bed that housed me and the light that greeted my waking. A huge debt of gratitude to my feet and legs that hit the floor. Oh yes, the floor that is but one in the home I love. Thanks for being the nest that I get to fluff day in and day out. Down the stairs to put on the tea pot . . . that's filled with clean water I needed only to turn on and place on a fire that was mine at the flip of switch. My heart overflows with gratitude.

But I am getting ahead of myself. If you are out and about the Twin Cities tomorrow and see a woman roaming the streets speaking thanks to stoplights and construction workers, smiling at orange-faced daylilies or geese swimming by, be kind. I am busy giving thanks.

Practice

Plan to offer your thanks generously today. Do so with words, spoken and written. Notice everything that sacrifices itself for your living. Offer your gratitude . . . liberally.

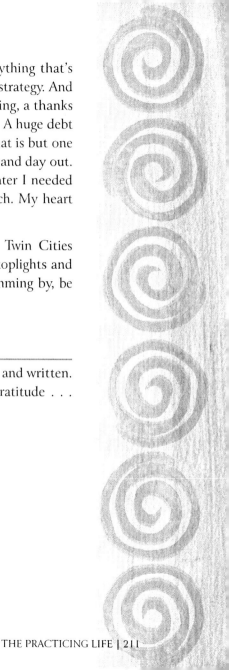

Overly Responsible

Late last week I found myself in blueberry heaven. Nestled in the rolling hills and rich, green valleys of southern Wisconsin lies Rush River Farm. It is a wonderfully idyllic place filled with row upon row of luscious blueberries and bright red currants. The white farmhouse and sturdy red barn welcome city immigrants to taste the goodness of farm living and working for a few hours at a by-the-pound fee. Colorful prayer flags fluttered in the breeze as pickers bent and reached between scratchy branches to turn their fingers blue with the fruit that hangs suspended in clean air and blazing sunshine. Conversations floated over the hedges, children's squeals and laughter danced in the air, and birdsong both real and recorded (to scare away the hungry winged ones) provided a soundtrack for our work. Looking out across the field a wide assortment of hats moved methodically down the perfect rows.

Picking berries is a kind of prayer for me. On Friday I was still in that place of "thank everything that is thank-able" that I lived earlier in the week. And so I was quietly thanking the plants and planters, the tenders, soil, water, and sun for providing this bounty. I was also thanking a Creator who dreamed up such a wild process by which we live, a process that calls us to be in tune with the often forgiving land that feeds us.

Picking can also be an obsessive kind of activity as I was reminded when a woman made her way down the row beside mine. Carrying her loaded-down basket of berries, she stopped to add a few more to the dark blue mound. "I just can't stop myself!" she said. "It is just greed, I guess." I affirmed that it is difficult to know when to stop. We laughed and she headed to check out. I returned to creating a larger pile of summer's abundance.

I thought then about her statement about greed and realized that for me it is not so much about greed. It is about responsibility. A responsibility to not waste any of the gift of this plant that offers itself to me. I want to save and enjoy each berry offered. What if no one comes who will pick this one? Or that one? What if they fall to the ground, uneaten, and die? Which, of course, some will. But that is a part of the whole amazing cycle of which human, plant, earth, and creatures are a part. What I am unable to pick will also become food for another human or the birds or insects or make its way into the soil as next year's fertilizer. It is a wonderful miracle.

Because I was still in that "thanking" place, I thought of Jesus' stories about farmers and seeds, not worrying or being overly responsible for things out of my control. I also thought about the psalmists, many of whom made their lives by being thankers: *"These all look to you to give them their food in due season; when you give it to them, they gather it up; when you open your hand, they are filled with good things. When you send forth your spirit, they are created; and you renew the face of the ground"* (Psalm 104).

I left my picking experience with several pounds of dark blue berries and a heart overflowing with gratitude. A gratitude that will be refueled each time I open the freezer and pull out a bag of fruit offered to me from the gifts of earth on an exquisite July morning. Thanks be to God!

Practice

To what do you feel responsible? In what ways do you recognize your connection to the gifts of the Earth? Notice today the food that is before you, the water that flows toward you. How can you connect more deeply with the miracle of this?

Hosta Heaven

What you gaze on, gazes back. What you contemplate in faithfulness, changes you into itself. Turning and turning you'll come around to being open like earth in which much can grow. – GUNILLA NORRIS

I began my morning with a stroll through a hosta heaven. I had taken the light rail to the office this morning which allows me to walk down Nicollet Mall and through the Loring Green area before making my way across Loring Park. As I progressed past the many green and manicured areas, between the high-rise apartments and condominiums, I began to notice the plethora of hostas. It is the boon of gardeners to plant hostas, those shade plants that allow a yard to have towering trees that create more shade than most flowering plants can take. These perennials have the magic of sprouting out in the spring and creating a blanket of green throughout the summer. All with very little work of the human kind! They are hearty and hardy plants and can grow with enthusiasm, needing only to be thinned out every so many years.

Along the pathway that curves and turns between the buildings, the landscapers have planted a wide variety of hostas. There are ones with white and green or yellow and green variegated leaves about the size of my palm. There are ones whose leaves shine in the light of any sun that manages to peak through the branches of the trees overhead. And then there are the ones whose leaves could almost conceal a small child, leaves tinged a Kentucky bluegrass color. Looking at them, one expects a fairy to emerge at any moment.

This was the path that began my day. I found that as I walked through these lovely shade loving plants, I began to walk more slowly. My eyes moved right, then left, careful not to miss any of the variety that had become a morning meditation. Snuggled between the hostas were flashes of color, impatiens and an occasional gerbera daisy. But the hostas held court in these green spaces created for the hungry, city soul. I allowed my pace to slow to what might be called meandering. There was work to get to, but walking through this heaven of hostas seemed the most important task at the moment. I found my spirits lift, my breath slow and go deeper.

There is much to admire about the hosta. It can flourish nearly everywhere. It is not a high maintenance flower. Basically you plant, water, and let it alone. It is one of the first green things to push up out of the soil in spring. It grows fast but not too fast, allowing those who really pay attention a certain satisfaction at its progress. If need be, it can spread to take up the space that is open. It does not need to be in the spotlight to be its true self. And when it overstays its welcome or spreads itself too far in any direction, it can be thinned out and given a new home to begin once again.

Sounds like a pretty good way to live to me. My invitation is this: The next time you have the blessing of being in the presence of a hosta, spend time with it, treasure its beauty and its strength, and learn from it. We could all do with being a little more hosta-like, don't you think?

Practice

Is there a plant or flower or other non-human being that inspires you? Perhaps it is a pet or wild bird outside your window. Spend time learning from something that can't talk to you . . . in words.

Drizzle

It has been a series of drippy, dreary days in Minnesota. The rain has at times been powerful and torrential and other times just drizzly, like a fine mist. Throughout it all the sun has been absent, the skies gray and gloomy. People are nearing the end of their collective ropes. Yesterday I was privy to the conversational comments of a few mothers of young children who had, much too soon, lost their lust for the summer vacation. Having been trapped inside for too long, their creative juices were drying up.

While I am now a fair distance from those days of trying to entertain children on rainy days or, even more importantly, trying to help them entertain themselves, I listened with a certain melancholy longing. A favorite video of our children was a quirky, little piece called "Drizzle and the Rainy Day." We actually rented this video when trapped inside a grandparent's house on several consecutive rainy days. It featured an odd, hairy puppet whose true gift was helping kids pass the time and have fun on rainy days. The trick with Drizzle was that the tools he used to do this were things already available in your house. I don't remember too many of the details except that things like empty toilet paper and paper towel rolls, straws and toothpicks became quite exciting creations. A little string, a marble, a Hotwheels car, and you had a racetrack or maze that wound its way from the living room couch, under the chair by way of the paper roll tunnels, through the dining room, out onto the kitchen floor, where it picked up speed and crashed into the dishwasher. The amount of time, energy, design, and redesign that went into these creations not only led to exercising imagination but, hopefully, to higher physics scores in high school.

I remember the Drizzle Days with great fondness. The sweet, simple joys of taking what was at hand for creativity and being entertained and challenged fill my heart, not only for the boys now turned men, but for the lazy days of making something out of nothing. Of course, this gift is available to us at all times, but sometimes it needs the imposition of rainy days to bear fruit. I have to admit that these gray, wet days have my mind turning to acts of creation much like a good, old-fashioned Minnesota blizzard. I am certain it doesn't work this way for everyone, but it does for me.

What weather brings out your creative spirit? What manner of sky can send you to paint a picture or write a poem or sing a song? What weather pattern can form around your days that leads you into that right-brained place that spins out new ideas faster than you can write them down? It is a good thing to understand your creative meteorology. When you know what fuels your creative spirit it becomes easier to see the inspiration as it begins to arrive. Yarn and needles call to be twisted and turned. Crayons and paper beckon from the closet where they have rested too long. The piano, silently sitting alone in the other room, begs to be played. That recipe you've wanted to try but took too long or needs too many ingredients shouts: "Now! Now!"

The rain will eventually lift and move on. So, those of us who have been trained in the Drizzle School need to get busy. Those of you guided by the Sunshine Way of creative thought, get plenty of rest tonight. Tomorrow the sun could to be moving in and next week the temperatures might rise as the skies clear.

There is much to be done . . . rain or shine!

Practice

Take stock of when you are most creative. Is your creativity driven by weather, time of day, season? Make a plan to pull out all the creative stops when the time is most right!

Holy Day

We seldom notice how each day is a holy place
Where the eucharist of the ordinary happens,
Transforming our broken fragments
Into an eternal continuity that keeps us. – JOHN O'DONOHUE

Sometime last week I read with interest a posting on a clergy friend's Facebook page which outlined what she had done that day. Its purpose was to answer an often asked question:" So, what do ministers do all day, anyway?" There are many folks, I'm sure, who think that a few hours a week in preparation for Sunday sermons is the extent of what might be on any clergy calendar. My friend's daily diary was impressive indeed as she listed the meetings attended, Bible study led, visits made, conversations had, more meetings, a stop in on the young children in the preschool, worship preparation, a luncheon meeting, and on and on into the evening. It was a whirlwind of purposeful, soulful activity. I smiled thinking of her moving through that most holy of days.

If we are awake and aware, each day is a holy day. And not just for religious "professionals." Each day holds the gift of communion, transformation, enlightenment, epiphany, even redemption. When I think about the day I have just lived, it held all this and so much more.

I began the morning having coffee with a friend and colleague. It had been my plan to simply catch up on her life and also check in on some worship details for a service she leads. But our conversation turned to challenging subject matter in which there was anger, disappointment, confession, absolution, and eventually deep understanding and love. This had certainly not been on my to-do list, had not been a part of my plan, but our time together became a gift of transformation that brought about an eventual feeling of freedom.

Lunchtime found me surrounded by some of our church's true saints. Every Wednesday two groups of worker bees gather at church. One threads needles and creates quilts for the crisis nursery and others who need the warmth of lovingly created comfort. The other picks up paint brushes and hammers and fix anything that needs to be fixed around the building. We, literally, would be a mess without them! I had been asked to offer the grace for their noontime picnic. As we ate our summer meal of hotdogs, brats, and potato salad, stories were shared of all the hours they have worked over nearly two decades together. Savoring my meal, I looked around the table and also noted who was no longer present, whose hands no longer painted or repaired. I had the sense that I was not the only one aware that while we were sharing a simple lunch we were also sharing a Meal of Memory.

A large portion of my afternoon was spent with our district superintendent as we looked back over the past year at goals I had set and what this year's work had been. OK, it was a kind of yearly job review. But in the course of our time together we shared our hopes and our frustrations with what it means to be this body called church. Having the opportunity to spew out all the good, the bad and the ugly of a year in one's life can be a humbling experience. Today I was privileged to eat the feast of humility and drink the cup of mercy.

These three events in my day were sandwiched between phone calls and emails, much like most working people. Also, like most people, I carried the brokenness and longing of my life into every word formed, every phone call answered, every conversation. It is holy work, this living. It is somehow made even holier when we take the time to notice the sacred threads that bind each moment together into a whole.

John O'Donohue ends this poem called "The Inner History of the Day":

So, at the end of the day, we give thanks
For being betrothed to the unknown
And for the secret work
Through which the mind of the day
And the wisdom of the soul become one.

We give thanks and look forward to the living of yet another holy day.

Practice

What is the holy work you will do today? Take a moment to notice the gifts within your conversations and encounters with those you know. What about the stranger? Look for ways in which the Spirit moves throughout your day. Name it. Claim it.

Getting Wet

Most of what we do in our worldly life is geared toward our staying dry, looking good, not going under. But in baptism, in lakes and rain and tanks and fonts, you agree to do something that's a little sloppy because at the same time it's also holy, and absurd. It's about surrender, giving in to all those things we can't control; it's a willingness to let go of balance and decorum and get drenched.

– ANNE LAMOTT, *Traveling Mercies: Some Thoughts on Faith*

We began our worship yesterday with these words. We laughed. It is very good now and then to begin worship with laughter. We do it so seldom. We laughed because most of us, the adults anyway, knew the truth of these words. Like most humans who can be open to knowing that the joke-finger is pointed in their direction, we joined forces in common laughter and a certain humility. Yes, each of us had spent considerable energy trying to "stay dry" in life.

But baptism was the central movement of our worship together. We were there to celebrate one of our little ones whose birth we had anticipated and then celebrated, whose personality we have been blessed to watch evolve. We have walked with her parents through these early months of her life and stand looking forward to watching her as she becomes. As we gathered to lay hands on her and to bless her with water combined from many sources, we all knew we were engaged in something holy and perhaps absurd. After all, who can understand it really? And yet, as humans, we try to cobble together the words that tell her and her parents that we are with them in this journey. Most importantly we all affirm once again that we believe the Holy travels with us. Even when we do not know it or understand what it means. Even when we don't feel as if we are worthy, or together enough, or even much of a "believer." Even when we don't get it or understand what it all might means. Even when our primary aim is to stay dry.

I know that throughout my life I have certainly spent a considerable amount of time and energy trying to stay dry and look good. I have probably also spent even more effort trying not to go under, not to send myself spiraling into a hole I feared I'd never crawl out of. I've twisted my self into shapes and knots only a contortionist should be able to do in order to keep control. Any of this sound familiar to you?

And yet, as Anne Lamott reminds us, this life we have been given is really mostly about surrender. The more we surrender to the surprises and unknowns, the more we allow ourselves to free fall into the Mystery that holds us. It is the dress rehearsal for the ultimate surrender we each reach at life's end. A daily practice of surrender can bring more than any of us could ever imagine and promises to keep our daily walk spicy and even exciting.

Baptism means many things to many people. But as I see it, this act we in the Christian household call a sacrament, is something visible to us of something that dwells within, whose ingredients are pure grace. Its action binds strangers and friends, guests and enemies, young and old, those who agree and those who argue, into a common, messy life together using that element of which we are all made and through which we are all sustained: water. Swimming through it all is the Creator whose image is imprinted on each of us.

Yesterday as we greeted this one so new to this messy, wonderful world, we did so with water and hope and love. "Come on in! The water is fine!" we said.

And so it is. And so it is.

Practice

Pour some water into a cup or bowl. Imagine what it is you want to surrender, let go, give up. Over this water, name what you want to surrender. Allow the water to absorb these things. When are you ready, pour this water out as you surrender and let go.

Pour Out Your Heart

There is a time between sleep and waking when dreams seem more vivid and the images planted in your resting brain become etched in profound ways. This is the time when you are not quite asleep and not quite awake, the time when you struggle to remember what day it is and where you are. It must be, in the Celtic tradition, a thin place of sorts, that place where this world and eternity coexist.

I had an experience of this in-between land this morning that I am still gently wrestling with. In the span of time between being unconscious and conscious, I heard this voice in my head: "Pour out your heart." I tried to come up from the darkened waters of sleep to connect these words with a dream I had been having, tried to attach the voice to some unknown being that played a part, opposite my own, in a nighttime drama. But I could not recollect any story that had been playing out in my sleep. Only the words: "Pour out your heart." The words seemed so significant that I even repeated them out loud to myself so I would not forget.

And now this message has been following me about all day. Pour out your heart. What could it possibly mean? Pour out my heart on what, to whom? What exactly am I supposed to be pouring from my heart? Compassion? Love? Empathy? I have to admit to feeling a little like the Kevin Costner character in "Field of Dreams" who kept hearing the voice saying, "Build it and they will come." He proceeded to plow over his Iowa cornfields and build a baseball diamond where dead but heavenly players came to play the game they had loved in life. But "pour out your heart" is a little less concrete than Kevin's baseball message. There is little direction other than the message itself.

But a good message it is. How could I go wrong pouring out my heart into every action I take? My work. My home. My family. My friendships. All the many things about which I feel passionate. There are also the small, seemingly unimportant acts that make up each and every day. Buttering toast. Drinking coffee. Loading the

dishwasher. Making the bed. Passing a stranger on the street. Setting the dinner table and eating with intentional gratitude. What about pouring heart into all that?

I have no idea why or how this message came to me. But it has given me much to ponder and consider on what could have been an otherwise ordinary day. But then again, if we pour our hearts into each day, can there even be such a thing as ordinary?

What a gift it was to have an early morning message that has so filled my day—with questions, with longing, with humor and hope, even, with God.

Practice

Are there words you'd like to guide your day? They need not be given to you in a dream. Think of what those words might be: breathe, slow down, smile, forgive. You decide. Take a pen and write the words on the palm of your hand. See what happens during the day.

Turtles

As I was preparing dinner last night, a report on the nightly news caught my attention. Apparently yesterday, in the midst of a busy day at New York's JFK airport, air traffic on some runways was halted due, not to threats of terrorism, but to the presence of turtles. Terrapins, to be exact. It seems the turtles were making their way across certain runways in pursuit of laying their eggs in the sand of Jamaica Bay which borders the airport. It also seems this is a yearly activity that has often played havoc with the comings and goings of jumbo jets and the pilots who fly them. It was fascinating to listen to the air traffic controllers and pilots, while they waited to take to the air headed toward far-flung places around the world, report to one another the progress of the lumbering turtles. To hear the humor and compassion in their voices was really quite remarkable.

For some reason it reminded me of my pilgrimage on the island of Iona. Before we began what was to be our three-and-a-half hour walk around the holy sites that dot the lovely isle, our guide reminded us: "Remember. On pilgrimage we travel at the pace of the slowest pilgrim." I watched as anxiety flashed across a few faces. Some in our group were quite fit and perhaps had seen this walk as exercise for the muscles and heart as well as the soul. But with the intention clearly stated, we journeyed on together, each learning to match our rhythm to one another until we became, not individuals, but a community of pilgrims. The walk actually took us nearly twice the time we had planned, but no one minded because we had come to know ourselves as now intricately woven together on this journey.

Thinking of the turtles and the wisdom gained in this pilgrimage experience, I pondered how often we forget about those who travel more slowly than our own pace. It becomes so easy to walk over or at least around them. I also thought about how often these days it seems we hold so little value for the sometimes smaller, more vulnerable around us. For those who live on the edges of our society, those

who need the care and attention of all who are stronger and have more resources. It becomes easy to push ahead with our powerful force, ignoring all that is in our way. We do this in a physical way sometimes, but mostly we do it with how we organize our common life together as neighborhoods, as cities, as nations.

The terrapins who are making their way across runways and past enormous metal people-movers do so for one reason: to bring life to the world. What endeavor is more noble, more holy than that? And so, for all the pilots, the baggage handlers, and the controllers who watched these slow moving beings make their own pilgrimage in the busiest airport in our country, I offer thanks. Thanks for your patience and self-control. Thanks for your compassion and humor. Thanks for remembering that on this pilgrimage we call life it is always a right and good thing to travel at the pace of the slowest pilgrim.

When we do, we are often offered the promise of new life.

Practice

Notice the speed at which different people move. Match your speed to theirs. What changes in you? How does it feel to move at the pace of another? Offer a prayer for all those who move slowly, who can use patience and gentleness this day.

Come, Rest Here

Yesterday I took advantage of the beautiful weather and walked around one of the Twin Cities many lakes. All the paths were crawling with people overjoyed to be outside their homes at last. Smiling people and equally happy dogs bounced along the walking paths. Strollers carrying joyful babies moved swiftly past runners and those roller blading as they soaked up sunshine and fresh air. Long stored bicycles now sported helmeted riders, using muscles they had forgotten they had. Each person seemed to be exercising the kind of freedom that is one of the true gifts of spring.

Nearing the end of my walk, I observed a biker taking over one of the many park benches that dot the lakeside. Sitting down, he called out to another biker still making their way along the path. "Come, rest here," he said. I looked to see the reaction of the receiver of these words. I wasn't close enough to really see, but it didn't really make a difference. I had already heard the invitation, and that was enough.

"Come, rest here." The words stuck in my mind. I thought of all the people who would welcome the gift of these three little words. Come. Rest. Here. Right here. I thought of the harried parent trying to juggle the myriad details of any given day. And the weary caregivers I know, dishing out food, compassion, patience, and love. I thought of the teachers and the restaurant workers and all the laborers who work long hours, often underpaid and under-appreciated. My memory was flooded with the many hospital workers I have occasion to see in action as I visit people who are ill or have had surgery. So many who would welcome this simple, calming invitation.

And then I thought of all the places, besides the park bench, that beckon us to "Come, rest here." All over this state docks will soon be moved into place and will take up their work of providing a resting place for those waiting to be healed by

the glassy, lapping water of being at "the lake." The front porch of my childhood, its glider, rocking chairs, and swing that are always present to create the slow, comforting motion we knew as infants in the womb. Back and forth, back and forth. Easy chairs and waiting room couches call out, "Come, rest here." Laps and outstretched arms offer children and loved ones that place of solace . . . come, rest.

In the Gospel of Matthew, Jesus goes about claiming a special relationship with God by saying to those gathered around him: "Come to me, all you that are weary and are carrying heavy burdens, and I will give you rest." What amazing and comforting words! And aren't they ones we have all, at one point or another, longed to hear?

For those of you who are weary and long for rest, may you have someone call out to you, like the biker on the bench, "Come, rest here."

May you find an invitation, even if it comes from your own lips, to sit, to be in the gift that is the present moment. And may you find rest there.

Practice

Create a place where you can rest, in your home or work place. Invite someone to join you with the words, "Come, rest here."

Too Sacred

If this world
Was not held in God's bucket
How could an ocean stand upside down
On its head and never lose a drop?
If your life was not contained in God's cup
How could you be so brave and laugh,
Dance in the face of death?
There is a private chamber in the soul
That knows a great secret
Of which no tongue can speak.
Your existence my dear, O love my dear,
Has been sealed and marked
"Too sacred," "too sacred," by the Beloved—
To ever end!
Indeed God
Has written a thousand promises
All over your heart
That say,
Life, life, life
Is far too sacred to
Ever end.
– HAFIZ, 1320-1389

Being held in God's cup seems a reassuring gift to me these days. I have found that sometimes the ways of the world weigh down my spirit and cause me to search for a way to come up from the dark waters that seem to rush over us, to find an opening where clear, clean air can rush into my constricted lungs. As I listen to

those in whom we have placed our confidence as leaders, take sides about how we give name and honor to those we love, I feel a sickened despair. When I think of the ways in which our nation allows fear to be our common food, I want to cry tears that will not stop. As I watch even our faith communities elevate violence to a sacrament and create laws that would exclude any of God's beloved ones, I wonder at what point we will cease our never-ending hurt of one another.

And so I have been doing what I find helpful. I have spent time talking with friends, friends who may not be in the low-riding valley of life's roller coaster right now. And I have been reading poetry and stories that weave beautiful phrases that lift my spirit. This poem of Hafiz did the trick. To be reminded of being held in God's cup brings a healing balm. And to reaffirm that deep goodness I believe exists within each of us is grounding. While not "preaching," that art that often contains too many words for me, poetry places just the right amount of syllables on my plate, allowing me to breath between the thoughts and find my way back to the home of myself.

This poem of the ancient Sufi mystic calls from someplace beyond time and wakes me up with his "too sacred, too sacred." Affirming that this life which we have been given by a loving Creator is too sacred to ever end is, for me, the wisdom of the Easter story. The assurance that no terror or fear ever plays the winning hand, that no harm we can ladle out or legislate ever ultimately prevails over the sacredness of life, allows me to breath more fully, to have an optimism that is choice, not logic.

Yesterday, a group of dear ones I call both colleagues and friends, lamented many of the same situations that have been nagging my spirit. We spoke of hope as choice. We spoke of making the choice to walk with hope into each day though we might have "considered the facts" as poet Wendell Berry writes. Perhaps we do this because we are all church "professionals" and we have been schooled in the ways of doing so. Perhaps we have decided to choose hope because we are of a certain age and to do otherwise would be simply too depressing.

But what I pray is that we have chosen hope because we know deep, deep down in that "private chamber of our souls" that the secret planted there, the secret of the sacredness of never-ending life prevails, and we can do nothing else but choose. Choose to hope. Choose to live up to the promises of God's imprint on our hearts. Choose to dance in the face of death. Choose to speak, act, vote, pray, and live this life which is "too sacred, too sacred" to do otherwise. And that we will live this way, not only for ourselves, but for all people, for all creatures, for all the world.

Practice

What allows you to choose hope? What person, place, or thing lifts your spirit with hope? Choose this day to spend your time in hope, with hope, full of hope, as an offering of hope.

Perpetual Apology

On Saturday morning I braved the gloomy weather and headed to the St. Paul Farmer's Market. It is one of the true pleasures of my week to begin my Saturday in this way. Even in these early days of the growing season I find myself undone by the beauty of vegetables, the color of flowers, the smells of brewing coffee, and the sight of so many different kinds of people. All up early. All shopping for food. Asparagus, spinach, and rhubarb shown forth as the "first to the market finish line." People were scooping up tiny tomato and basil plants as they dreamed of the bruschetta that will come in July. Children, and some adults, munched on sugary, sprinkled donuts as we chose not to notice the gray, rainy skies.

Instead of a donut, I opted for a toasted pumpernickel bagel. While I was waiting for it to take a turn on the grill, I watched the young adults who work this booth. They wore the Saturday morning sleepy look of most their age. A look that belies a too late night followed by a too early morning. But they laughed and joked with one another, showing the camaraderie they have developed in this job that will lead them to something else, i.e. a tuition payment, rent for another month, enough spending money for another late night.

In my scanning of these young people, my eyes fell on one young man, his black hoodie unzipped to reveal a dark gray t-shirt. And then I saw the tattoo that formed a ring on his neck. Moving from left to right, across the sinking place on his white, fragile skin were the dark blue, elegant letters that said simply: "I am so sorry." For some reason these words hit the pit of my stomach and didn't bounce back. What could this young man be so sorry about that he had this tattooed forever on his neck where all would see? Why had he made so permanent this perpetual apology? These questions seared through my brain as another young woman handed me my warm bagel oozing with cream cheese. As I walked away I felt my heart tug for him.

All day I thought of this quick encounter with someone I may never see again but whose bodily adornment had so moved me. The words on his neck caused me to think of all the situations, all the actions in the world for which I am so sorry. I thought of all the people I come into contact with during a given week who are homeless or living on the edge. I am so sorry that as a nation we cannot figure out how to keep people from falling through the cracks of our social systems. I am so sorry that we continue to engage in hate and fear-filled actions that threaten to marginalize people on the basis of whom they love. I am so sorry that we continue to lash out at those whose faith is foreign to us, those who appear different because of the ways they dress or speak or even eat. I am so sorry that children and the elderly often are the recipients of the actions of a few making decisions for the many. So much to be sorry about. This young man took, in my opinion, a radical and permanent way of living this.

It is easy to get lost in "sorry." But somehow it seems to me the gentler thing, not only individually but communally, is to try to get at the front end of apology. To try to take a breath before acting, before speaking so as to cut down on the need for perpetual apology. In some ways it is an impossible intention but also a noble one. Even in our communal life to ask ourselves, as the prophet Micah did, "What does God ask of you?" To ask and then to shape our lives around the answer: "Do justice, love kindness, walk humbly with God." How might our need for apology be changed if these values guided our actions? It is something to ponder.

I am thankful for the toasty bagel that fed my body on Saturday morning and the hands that prepared it. And I am thankful to the young man whose message has traveled with me and will continue to nudge me to be careful with my words, my actions, and my life. The pain he must have endured to wear the words he carries as a mantra was not lost on me.

Wherever he is, may God bless his path this day.

Practice

Have you ever considered a tattoo? If you have one, what led to your choice? If you decided to have words tattooed as a message to the world, what might your message be? Walk through the day as if those words are already visible to the world.

Mystics

The day of my spiritual awakening was the day I saw,
and knew I saw, all things in God and God in all things.
— MECHTILD OF MAGDEBURG

In preparation for Sunday's worship, I have been searching through several books of writings by Christian mystics. Each time I come upon the words of those who have tried to express in words their deep experience of the Holy, I find myself once again flooded with humility. So many of those we now speak of as mystics lived at times when it must have been truly dangerous to speak many of the things they did. While many men fall into this category, an equal number are women, also a humbling and amazing fact.

What does it mean to be a mystic? Most definitions point toward someone who has great intuition that leads to a spiritual truth, one that allows a communion with God, which is often brought about by meditation or deep contemplation. From that definition it might seem as if there are few, if any, mystics among us these days. But I don't believe that is the case.

In the first place, many children are mystics. Have you taken a walk with a child lately? Have you watched them spend time with, say, an ant hill? Squatting next to a child and an ant hill can make a mystic out of the most logical person. The questions they ask, the insights they have could fill a hundred books. If you want to have a mystical experience, invite a child to accompany you on a walk in a park or in the woods. Let them set the pace, stopping at every interesting stone, feather, tree, flower, animal print. Children are our first teachers that God is present in all things. Each of us were teachers once too, but along the way we may have forgotten to stop, to look, to listen, to know the Holy One's movement in the everyday acts of our living.

Spring is a particularly good time to hone one's mystic skills. Walking out on any given morning, it becomes nearly impossible to miss God showing up everywhere. The pink and drooping bleeding hearts can offer infinite wisdom about fleeting beauty. The rich, piercing fragrance of lilies-of-the-valley can settle on our spirits and stir us to memories of times we were held close by perfumed, fleshy, grandmother arms. The strong and powerful push of hostas once more making an entrance into the world teach us of an abiding presence and endurance which holds us through cold, frozen, even difficult times.

Mechtild of Magdeburg was a medieval mystic who lived in Germany in the thirteenth century. Her mystical experiences of God were described in her book *The Flowing Light of Divinity*. She was often known to be critical of church authorities and doctrines and the ways in which the church often tried to reign in the Sacred. Instead she described her encounters of the Divine in all things and how all things are at the same time held in the Divine. It is fascinating to me that she was allowed to live and write and speak. After her death, for more than 400 years her writings were suppressed. But over the last years her words, like so many mystics, have made their way into wider circles. Perhaps they are the very words we need for the times in which we live.

Have you had an encounter with the Holy recently? Have you shared it with anyone? Have you spent time looking at an ant hill or a bird's nest or the irises that are waiting for just enough sunshine to bloom? We were born as mystics, I believe. The experience of the Sacred is just a breath away. If we take our time, honor the gift of the moment, and remember to act like a child.

Practice

If possible, spend time outside with a child today. If this is impossible, spend time alone truly observing the world. Take the time to focus on a specific tree or flower or body of water. Make note of what you experience of the Holy while being present to these gifts of Creation. Tell someone about it.

Responsible

Alright. I admit it. I rushed home from the office yesterday to watch the final episode of "Oprah." Off and on over the years I have tuned into this show and have watched the gradual transformation of, not only the show, but the woman. I have admired the ways in which Oprah encouraged a pursuit of reading and the birth of book clubs and conversation around the interpretation of books. I have often seen her speak boldly to people who needed it and be gracious and kind to those who most would have turned their backs. I have been amazed at her generosity. I would only hope that if such fortune ever came my way, I would be as gracious and thoughtful with my resources. With others, I have watched her battle the demon of weight control and seen the inspiration she has been to so many.

People may disagree with me, but what I have come to see, to believe, is that Oprah grew into a fine preacher. She used words like "calling" and "redemption" and "transformation" in ways most Sunday morning preachers do. But she was heard in a different way. From the safety of the brightly colored, soft and comfy living room set, she spoke of God, even Jesus, without seeming to exclude anyone. She was always upfront about it. Never apologized for speaking about her faith to what she knew was her diverse audience. She spoke of the hardship of her life while welcoming others to do the same. She also spoke openly of the privilege that she now has and how she understands her responsibility to be a good steward of what has come her way. I often watched as she used the tools of any good preacher to bring people to a deeper understanding of a topic but mostly of themselves.

On her final show she graciously spoke of all that the audience had given her. One of the most profound sections of the show recounted a woman who had a stroke and was unable to speak. The woman was a psychologist and told of how the doctors had come into her room and spoke about her as if she wasn't there, saying things that no thoughtful person would say in the presence of another if

they thought the person could hear. Contrasted were her family and friends who spoke words of encouragement as they surrounded her with love and compassion. Through this experience the woman, who is now recovered, spoke of how each of us are energy, vibrant electrical beings, who carry the ability to affect others in negative and positive ways. She had given Oprah a large card that had been hanging in her makeup room. It simply said: *"Please be responsible for the energy you bring into the room."*

When Oprah reported these words, words which had come to guide not only her but her staff, I reflected back on all the times I have been in a meeting where the energy in the room was so negative it seemed impossible to do good work of any kind. I thought about the times when I have been surrounded by the energy of people who are so loving and caring it seemed we all might levitate. I was reminded of the times I have carried negative, hurtful energy into a situation only to have the gathering implode before my very eyes.

We are all energy, and we carry energy into every encounter, every meeting, every relationship, every conversation. It is an awesome responsibility if we take it seriously—to consider the way *our* energy, the energy of each human being, is helping to bring healing and hope this day. I truly believe none of us would want to carry an energy that would have the power to hurt another.

So perhaps today, this minute, is the time to print these words on our doors, on the palms of our hands, on our fragile hearts: *"Please be responsible for the energy you bring into the room."*

Practice

What kind of energy are you carrying today? Is it energy that will serve the world for good? Or will it cause more harm to an already troubled time? Perhaps it is time to take stock.

Stirring

This year Holy Saturday, the day before Easter, coincides with the anniversary of my father's death. I had not actually thought much about this fact until this week when I have been living with the words and messages of this day, Maundy Thursday. In worship services everywhere we will once again remind people of Jesus gathering with his friends in what we have come to call the Upper Room. This story is woven throughout with the humility of Jesus. It is in this room where he washes the feet of his friends, and they share in the Last Supper.

Perhaps I am thinking of my dad because pretty much everything I have come to know about humility I learned from him. He was also a man who loved to eat and to share food with those he loved. He was happiest when food was plentiful and people were filling their plates with the bounty. He moved quietly in the world, and I don't think I ever heard him say a bad thing about another person. I only wish I could say I inherited this trait. But I will say, when I find myself forming what could be hurtful words, I often hear my dad's breath moving someplace near my ear as an unseen censor. It is a blessing.

There are other times, of course, when I am reminded of my dad and the important, though understated and quiet, presence he had in my life. The sound of a radio announcer's voice as a baseball game is being played conjures up memories of hot summer nights and the muffled calling of a Cincinnati Reds game wafting from my parent's bedroom late at night. The sight of pie, nearly any pie, his favorite dessert. Once a quick turn of my head as I observed our oldest son standing with arms crossed over his chest, listening intently to a conversation, carried a resemblance to my dad that took my breath away. And being in the presence of our younger son whose gentle ways often remind me so much of his grandfather, make me smile a knowing smile. These are all visceral moments of deep memory.

Poet Annie Breitenbucher has a phrase in a poem: "It stirs your ashes in the bowl of my heart." It is a lovely, poignant image, isn't it? All these experiences and memories are "stirring the ashes in the bowl of my heart" today.

A small cherry bush is planted in our front yard as a memorial gift from friends, a gift to commemorate my father's life. In the first two years of its living in our yard it actually bloomed on the anniversary of his death. It seemed a miracle to me. The next spring, like this one, followed a too harsh winter, and there were no lovely pink blossoms to mark the day. That spring I felt an agitation and impatience that nearly undid me. But this year I have seen it coming. There have been no visible buds until the last few days. Hopefully, with the warm weather this weekend, progress will be made and blossoms will soon be bursting with hope and memory.

Tonight as we gather to remember the life of Jesus, his humility, and his acts of hospitality and service, I will be present to the story that is being told, the telling of "love before dust." But I will also be holding in my heart the love returned to dust that continues to stir, bringing memory and definition to my life. What has not yet blossomed will be made known in its own time, and for that my heart is very full.

Practice

Create the time and space to bring to memory those you have loved and lost. Say their names aloud and allow those names to hover in the air. Allow the memory of their presence to be a reminder of their life. Give thanks.

New Heaven

No pessimist ever discovered the secrets of the stars, or sailed to an uncharted land, or opened a new heaven to the human spirit. – HELEN KELLER

Leafing through a book today, I ran across this quote. Normally I gloss over things like this. I wasn't searching for it necessarily but I found it anyway, or perhaps it found me. Perhaps the words found me so they could give me a good swift kick in the pants. I needed to be jarred into my truer self. The self that doesn't carry a little tin of pessimism in my pocket ready to be hauled out at the slightest notice. I am not by nature a pessimistic or negative person but I have found this little cloud of "yuckiness" that has been following me about lately. Much like that old Cream of Wheat commercial where the bowl of healthy, steaming cereal follows the child from breakfast table to the bus and on to school. Nutrients swooping in to fill stomach and brain throughout the school day!

My shadow bowl has not been so healthy or nutritious. Instead I have allowed my spirit to be dragged down by heavy, unhelpful thoughts to the point where I realized I have been going, for what seems like a very long time, without breathing. I have realized that I have been walking around so deep in my thoughts that the center of my being seems to be my furrowed forehead instead of my heart. Has this ever happened to you?

I have spent some time reflecting on how this state of mind, this way of being came to take up residence. Partly I am sure that I am simply mirroring the culture around us all. The negative and pessimistic opinions and words of the news and the world fly around and land like bad fairy dust, settling on shoulders and eyelashes and seeping into our brains. It becomes difficult not to be weighed down by it all, not to allow it to wriggle its way into turning us all from hopeful people who have a potential to help heal the world into naysayers who cannot be amazed at the secrets of the stars or the excitement of visiting an uncharted land.

As a person of faith, I believe we have great potential to help open up a new heaven to the human spirit. The story of Easter tells that, in the midst of what seemed like a terrible tragedy, new life sprang forth to change lives forever. The sacred texts of most traditions continue to reaffirm similar life-giving stories. Pessimism rarely wins and never, in my experience, feels very good, nor is it easy to continue for long periods of time without burning out or burning up.

So, right now I am choosing to breathe. Breathe deeply and allow the goodness that is the air filling my lungs remind me of this precious life through which I am blessed. I am going to imagine another bowl, a different one, following me around for the next several days. A bowl overflowing with the life-giving nourishment of compassion, love, peace, hope, joy, and kindness toward myself and everyone I meet. I am going to fill my belly with its goodness and be about the work of healing the world. One spoonful at a time. Over and over again until my own human spirit catches a glimpse of that new heaven. If you too have been eating a bowlful of negative mush, I invite you to join me.

Practice

In a time of quiet, take stock of your own mood. Is it one of healthy optimism or pessimism? Take some time to reflect on what has caused your current mind and heart set. Imagine a bowl hovering above your shoulder that is full of whatever you need to move into a better place. Take a bowl in your hands and drink what you need.

✐ransitions

After six days of waking every morning to the singing of birds and sun and warm air flowing through our window, we will prepare to make a transition back from California to Minnesota. Tomorrow we will load our warm weather wardrobe into the suitcases, tuck the stones and shells collected as souvenirs into soft spaces for protection, and head back to the newly fallen snow that awaits us. In some ways we have received the gift of a glimpse of the spring that is to come . . . minus the sand and palm trees, of course. We have had a little break from pulling on layer upon layer and stuffing our feet into shoes that are completely utilitarian. With an assurance of what is to come, we will be privileged to come home and see the slow, gentle emergence of color, flowers, birdsong, and new life that is only a few weeks away.

I was thinking about this transition as we walked yet another beach today. We had set the goal of visiting a different beach every day, and we achieved our goal. Today's beach, Coronado Beach, is graced by the exquisite Hotel de Coronado, whose white exterior and red roofs make a stunning statement on this stretch of the Pacific Ocean. We walked along watching children running and laughing as parents looked on from their beach chairs. Students wrapped in towels, perhaps on spring break, read books as they soaked up the much-needed sun. One older gentleman was creating an amazing sand castle. Overhead jets flew low, making an incredible noise as they executed maneuvers and headed back toward their base. It was a rich and beautiful scene which I reveled in soaking up.

And then I saw them. Three pairs of shoes lined up in a row heading out toward the water. The first pair situated nearest the land was a pair of brown winter boots. There they sat, empty, as if the owner had been lifted skyward out of their heavy leather so full of purpose. Within a few feet another pair of shoes stood in line, also

empty, with no owner in sight. Running shoes. They were neatly positioned in line with the boots as if the wearer had discarded the boots and made their way into the freedom of these fast-moving fliers.

But the topper was what came next in the lineup. A pair of flip flops sat even nearer to the waiting ocean. Boots. Running shoes. Flip flops. All lined up as if the wearer had gone from one to the other in the speed of a California minute. I laughed out loud at the thought of it.

Every time I visit a place where the seasons are not as pronounced as they are in my own world, I wonder what it might be like to have fewer times of transition. What is it like to have a more temperate climate for the majority of the year? What is it like to have fresh fruit and vegetables that have not traveled more than a few miles most of the time? Certainly those who live here notice changes that would be invisible to my nonnative eyes. Those who live in places where four seasons are not as pronounced may not notice the subtleties of the transition of winter to spring, spring to summer, summer to fall, fall back to winter. We all learn to see and know what the play of light is like in our own backyards, and there is gift in being both native and guest.

I have worn sandals much of this week, and my running shoes will carry home some of the sand that got buried in the tread as we fulfilled our goal of walking many beaches. But by Saturday morning my feet will be tucked back into my snow boots until it is time to make the transition. It will come when the time is right . . . and not a minute before, I'm sure.

Practice

What transitions are happening for you right now? In what way can you honor these transitions? Light a candle and say your prayers of hope and longing for the transitions that are being offered.

Hidden Treasure

Several days of every week I have evening meetings. On these days, that may have started early in the morning with other responsibilities, I always try to take a little break around 4:00 to clear my head, get some fresh air, and have a little sabbath time. I often head to a lovely little bakery restaurant in the Uptown area where I hug a cup of coffee and allow the chocolate in one of the best chocolate chip cookies known to humanity melt in my mouth. Yesterday was one of those days that stretched over many hours, and so I headed out to engage in this sacramental moment.

It goes without saying that driving and particularly parking your car anywhere these days is a challenge. The snow has now built up so high that most humans need to take on a mountain goat approach to nearly every curb and intersection. Driving, I made my way along the ever-narrowing streets and safely maneuvered around corners where snow was piled higher than my car. Safe sight lines have now gone the way of the streetcar. I parked with the curb side of the car elevated on ice-impacted snow and toppled out of the car.

Bundled up against the freezing wind, I made my way around to the parking meter. From the sidewalk there was a small path cut into the boulevard by the feet of all those who had gone before me. They must have been small people—unusually small people with equally small feet—because I had to stand with one foot in front of the other as I balanced on the snowbank. I did not feel like a dancer in this ballet-like position. My mittened hands now had to reach into my wallet to retrieve the quarters which would feed the meter so I could have the chocolate chip cookie that had become my prize. Fumbling with a mitten in one hand, my exposed flesh held two quarters as I balanced like a flamingo. One quarter slid easily into the meter, but somehow the balancing or the wind chill caused the second quarter to slide in a free fall from my fingers into the snow below. I watched it fall slowly down as my eyes followed it. Looking at the snow below I saw the

slice it had made in the snow. And surrounding it were several other identical slices—quarters that had fallen as others had balanced in the same place, quarters that will lie hidden in the snow until the spring thaw.

I laughed and wanted to tag this meter so some lucky person will know to watch for the treasure that will emerge. As I plugged in another quarter and headed inside for my now much-deserved treat, I began to think of all the hidden treasures that are waiting to emerge from these winter days. Ruminating over my warm coffee and delicious cookie, I watched the people move by outside, the life of them visible in the breath that surrounded their heads, that blew forth from their red faces. Each is carrying a treasure that is also perhaps hidden. Under the frozen ground all kinds of bulbs and seeds are resting and waiting for the right moment to begin to make their way toward life anew. I observed a couple meeting with a real estate agent as they dreamed of a new home that will no doubt be filled with the treasures of their lives. Sitting near by a young woman wrote passionately on her computer. What treasure lies hidden within the words she so furiously meted out?

Most often we think of treasures as monetary. But in the book of Matthew, the teacher Jesus reminds the people that "*where your treasure is, there your heart will be also.*" What do you treasure? What treasures lie hidden within you that long to be brought out into the light of day? What treasure, if discovered, would make your heart sing?

Today may find us balancing in places that don't feel so comfortable, or at least not very graceful. The winds may be rushing around the doors of life exposing our vulnerabilities. But there are treasures we carry and ones that are just outside our vision that will be revealed . . . often in their own good time, when the melting is over. Our work is, most often, to practice patience and openness in the waiting.

But for someone with a really good shovel and strong arms, there are quarters to be had beneath a parking meter in Uptown!

Practice

Make a list of what it is you treasure. Spend time reflecting on this list. Allow the feelings of these revelations to make your heart sing.

Baggage

On many Sundays, I remind those with whom I worship that we have all arrived with the bags of our week carried invisibly at our sides. Indeed, we carry the bags of our lives fully packed with us through every moment of every day. It is a helpful metaphor, a useful image for me as I assess the sometimes curious reasons why I do what I do. It is something I tell couples I meet with as we do pre-marriage counseling. They carry with them the bags of the lives they have led up to that point, and they will carry the contents of those bags into this life they will forge together. It is true, I believe, of all relationships, all friendships. The baggage of our life thus far infuses our work, our play, our understanding of faith, the development of what we might even call our theology.

So, it was with some fascination that I read a prayer today from a little prayer book published by the Iona Community. It was written by Kathy Galloway.

> *Oh my Lord,*
> *I am carrying too much luggage,*
> *and it's weighing me down,*
> *holding me back.*
> *I worry about losing it,*
> *but don't need much of the stuff I'm dragging about.*
> *It blocks up the aisles and gangways,*
> *getting in the way,*
> *making people cross*
> *and wrapping itself around my ankles.*
> *I need to travel light,*
> *but don't know what to do with all this stuff.*

Whew! I can certainly relate to those words. Can you? I think of all that is packed in my bags: guilt, old resentments, unfair expectations of myself and others, jealousy, feelings of being wronged or misunderstood, insecurities to beat the band, failures . . . the list goes on and on.

Of course I also have some very fine stuff packed that I carry with me all the time. The felt experience of unconditional love, the support of community, deep friendships, a sense of humor, the love of beauty, to name only a few. I think of some of those things I am glad I have packed away, things like my father's gift of loyalty passed on to me through DNA and modeling. I treasure it. And yet I also know that even this precious, positive gift has sometimes kept me blind to important realities, kept me closed to some possibilities.

How we are able to understand the luggage we carry makes a big difference in how we move and have meaning in the world. What we have packed in our bags has the power to move us forward or hold us back.

Kathy Galloway's prayer ends with these words:

> *Here,*
> *you take it.*
> *I'm leaving it with you.*
> *Perhaps you can find a better use for it.*
> *For who knows me better than you,*
> *who has given me the substance of my life,*
> *bone and marrow, patterned in my mother's womb?*
> *You are my unfolding and my unburdening.*
> *You are the keeper of my deepest secrets.*

For all which we carry with us every day that needs honoring, may we find the grace to do so. For all that needs to be given away or given up, may we have the courage to unloose our grip. All the while knowing the Holy One walks with us in each blessed step.

Practice

What is packed in your bag? What are you ready to throw out to lighten your way? Decide what is tucked away in your life's luggage that no longer serves you. To travel lighter, toss it!

Prayer Search

I did not know it. But I have been searching for prayer. After the groundedness of Advent and the flurry of Christmas, I entered this season of Epiphany much like the Magi . . . searching. I found myself wandering from bookshelf to bookshelf. Leafing through poems, devotions, digging out bits and pieces of theological candy. But in the end, I was left still hungry. It was frustrating and confusing.

And then Friday I headed to a local store that caters to "all things churchy." Candles, vestments, music, and books. I found myself roaming around, somewhat aimlessly, until I landed in the section labeled prayer. I began to look around at the various books and felt something move inside me. Like the Wise Ones who traveled through the desert, the Star had led me to a treasured place. I began to read the pages filled with prayers and words about prayer from various perspectives. Prayers from other traditions. Prayers for those who wanted a deep, spiritual practice. Prayers for women. Prayers to color. Prayers to read aloud with others. I walked out of the store with four books that seemed to bring something hopeful to my search.

Now I don't hold any illusions that these prayers written by others will completely fill this longing I feel. But they may be a start. Like Mary Oliver who wrote: *"I don't know what a prayer is, but I do know how to pay attention,"* I am paying attention to this gnawing at my core that will not let me go. I am paying attention to the Holy trying to communicate with me. I am trying, trying to listen.

This morning as I sat, coffee cup in hand, preparing for a little quiet time before my day began, I reached for one of the books I had purchased on Friday. *"Where does this deep down, soulful hunger come from? The ache that you and I experience deep in our souls was created by the One in whose image we are made. We are meant for God and God is meant for us,"* writes author Dan Schutte. In the fullness of this day, with

all its beauty and its violence, I am holding out that prayer can and does make a difference. And with each breath, I will continue paying attention and . . . searching.

Practice

Using these words as a breath prayer, prayer while inhaling "we are meant for God" and exhaling "God is meant for us." Continue breathing quietly and slowly while these words find a home in you.

Imperfection

This week I began reading *The Spirituality of Imperfection* by Ernest Kurtz and Katherine Ketcham. It is a book my clergy support group has chosen for an upcoming retreat. I am really only a few pages into the book and already can see that this is going to one that is marked mightily with my pen and highlighter. Sentences like:

> *Spirituality teaches us, or has taught most of us, how to deal with failure. We learn at a very young age that failure is the norm in life . . . errors are part of the game, part of its rigorous truth."* And: *"Spirituality begins with acceptance that our fractured being, our imperfection, simply is: There is no one to 'blame' for our errors—neither ourselves nor anyone nor anything else. Spirituality helps us first to see, and then to understand, and eventually to accept the imperfection that lies at the very core of our human be-ing.*

And all that is only in the introduction! In beginning this book I was reminded of a not too distant time when then word "spirituality" used in mainline churches made people quite nervous. What did it mean? How was it different from religion? What did it look like to be spiritual? How was what happened in church spiritual . . . Or not?

But over the years even the most mainline of mainlines have come to a certain comfort, if not outright acceptance, of the word spiritual. It now shows up in most church newsletters and may even creep into a sermon or two. While its definition may still be elusive to some, there is a sense that being spiritual is simply something we are. Something we are in all our imperfections, not in spite of them.

As humans we have this bent toward pursuing perfection. It is present in so much of our culture and drives the advertising that engulfs us. Perfect bodies, perfect relationships, perfect jobs, perfect homes. This list goes on and on. Indeed, United

Methodists speak of "going on to perfection," a statement woven into our fabric by our founder John Wesley. The fact that he was speaking of wholeness often is lost on the hearer given how ingrained that pursuit of perfection is in our common language. Just talk to any therapist, and it will become obvious how deep the chase for perfection runs within us.

Yet every morning we each awake with the failures of yesterday painted in our cells and dripping off our skin. It is simply a fact. Some of us carry more paint, more drips than others. But no one, no one is immune. And someplace in that drippy paint that covers us, we can, if we choose, come to know the Spirit that moves in it all. The Spirit that does not expect us to be perfect but to be a human be-ing. It is a vulnerable place to be, a vulnerable relationship to develop. But in truth it is, I believe, the only way to move through the world. Daily wearing our vulnerability, our humanness, our imperfection like the images of God we are.

The authors of *The Spirituality of Imperfection* include in their introduction a small story I have heard often and love more each time I hear it. It originally comes from a work of the great theologian Martin Buber: *"Rabbi Zusya said, "In the coming world, they will not ask me, 'Why were you not Moses?' They will ask me, 'Why were you not Zusya?'"*

And so it is. Perfection, however we define it, in whatever way we pursue it, is not really our work. Our work is to embrace the fullness of our imperfection with all its gifts and failures. Our work is to become the fragile, fractured human we are. It is joyful and painful work. It is spiritual work.

Practice

Check your pulse for the ways of perfection. Where can you say no? Where an you be gentle with yourself?

Smiling

When I smiled at them, they scarcely believed it;
the light of my face was precious to them. – JOB 29:24

Yesterday people were once again stocking up at grocery stores in preparation for another predicted snowstorm. It is an intriguing process that never ceases to surprise me. After all the years I have lived in Minnesota, to see people filling store parking lots in order to make sure they have enough bread, milk, chocolate . . . whatever seems to be the needs for being sequestered to your house while snow falls and winds blow as we wait for the plows to do their work. It is fascinating. In today's light, the snow really is more steady than falling fast, but the colder temperatures make it more dangerous for driving. To have labeled it a storm may have been dramatic.

For many people this kind of weather brings out their dour, "I'm tired of this" face. So this morning, as I read a small article in the paper about what you can do to put a smile on your face, I thought of all those who woke up today with a prepared frown. The article listed ten things you can do to add that needed lift of the lips. It included things like cooking a wonderful meal and visiting an animal shelter to pet something furry. There were easy ideas like getting dressed up to do regular acts of your day. The thought is we always feel better when we know we look nice. The one that made me laugh was "organize your sock drawer." Having just done this recently, I know the odd feeling of freedom and accomplishment this simple little task brings. I am not sure having done so made me smile, but it made me feel more orderly, which is a good thing, I guess. There were several other good ideas on the list including a YouTube video that featured the song "Stand by Me."

The exercise someone took on to create this list piqued my curiosity and caused me to begin to think of those things that actually make me smile. I'd like to offer a few ideas of my own. Things that over the last few days lifted me from the doldrums of a very, snowy winter.

Dance with a baby. I did this yesterday at church. While beautiful jazz music sealed the ending of our worship, I lifted my arms out to one of our newly walking members. Her soft, pudgy fingers joined my rough, dry ones, and we swayed to the music as she looked deeply into my eyes with all the wonder and curiosity of her freshness on the earth. I carried the memory of her, our dancing, with me all day, creating a perpetual smile. The sheer act of holding her aliveness lifted my spirits.

Let the snowflakes fall on your tongue. Catch them as you did when you were a child and make a note that you, a unique creation, are swallowing an equally unique creation. There is something to all that uniqueness savoring uniqueness which brings a smile to my face.

Spend time looking out a window. Narrow your view for a few minutes and let the vast worries of the world fall away. For a few moments give thanks for all you can see out the limited view of your window. The children waiting for the bus (say a prayer for them). The mounds of snow that have now become near icebergs. The tracks of a rabbit that kept watch outside while you were sleeping. Where is it now? Is it watching you, hidden from your human eyes, as you look out through your refined vision?

Every day brings with it many worries, many sorrows. Every day also brings the potential for lifting our spirits, for taking stock of the joyful moments that are gift to us. As we exercise our face muscles we generate endorphins that nourish us, maybe even adding a few moments to our longevity. Sounds worth it to me. The dark of winter may feel as if it is holding us hostage. But we have the power to lift ourselves above the drifts with the beauty of an upturned smile.

Practice

What puts a smile on your face? How can you create more of those experiences that feed your smiling spirit? Make a list. Refer to it often. Add to it each new, grinning observation.

Birds

You won't be able to control your thoughts. They are like birds that fly from your grasping hands. But if you relax, those birds may perch on your shoulder, and then you can walk, taking them where you want them to go. – HOROSCOPE, DECEMBER 8

When I opened the paper this morning and read my horoscope, I didn't so much laugh as I felt resigned, perhaps even redeemed. Redeemed from a night when sleep would not come. Or at least would not come at the "proper" time. This is the second night this week when I have done battle with my eyelids. A night earlier I also had bizarre sleeping patterns, finally getting up at four in the morning and giving in to the circling thoughts that kept my mind too busy for sleep.

I am normally a "very good sleeper" just as I am a "very good eater." I listen with all the compassion I can muster to many of my friends who struggle with insomnia. The nutritional and physical gymnastics they go through to get a good night's sleep frankly exhaust me. But last night, when my brain would not stop its work, I began to feel a kinship with them like never before. I can chalk it up to stress, the general work load that is December, the pattern of the moon, what I ate, what I didn't eat. But mostly I think it was a mixture of creativity and anxiety.

The creativity comes from many projects that are in a state of transition, dreamed but not yet in motion or realized. The anxiety comes from the same source, big thoughts that are swimming in my gray matter but not yet fully formed. Ever had this experience? The difficulty with not being able to turn that part of your brain off for the sake of sleep is that, in the nocturnal state, our vulnerability begins to add all the other worries we carry just below surface. The little pain becomes something grave. The door we see opening suddenly smacks shut. The people we are sure of in our waking hours can seem less our allies in the fog of sleeplessness.

So in this hyper-thought place, I decided to do the only thing I knew how to do. I began being present to my own breath. Holding myself as still as possible, I began riding the wave of the energy that gives me life. Soon I realized that my breathing had become a prayer: "Let sleep come. Let sleep come. Let sleep come." The Spirit and I had come to an agreement, and we were co-existing.

The Buddhists refer to my nighttime experience as "monkey mind." But today's horoscope gave me a different image, one I find helpful. Birds. The thoughts which were flying around could have been the harbingers of creativity that need a nest in which to rest. My real work is to relax enough, to breathe deeply enough, to allow them to perch on my shoulders so I can hear their song.

Are they doves? Crows? Chickadees? Cardinals? I'm not sure. But if today . . . or tonight . . . finds you unable to focus the gifts of your thoughts, I invite you to imagine these invisible throngs allowing them to become companions. Companions with wings set to travel with you through the ups and downs of this day.

Who knows what message they might deliver, what song they might sing?

Practice

Wherever you are and whatever the tasks of your day, spend time paying attention to your breath. Notice what you need to be present to the work or people you encounter. Breath a message to yourself that helps bring you into the present moment.

Amidst Life's Dark Streaks

For the first showings of the morning light
and the emerging outline of the day
thanks be to you, O God.

– J. PHILIP NEWELL, *Celtic Benediction: Morning and Night Prayer*

Yesterday, I began my day with this prayer. I sat at a neighborhood coffee shop having my warm cup of coffee, staring into the middle distance at the cars and people rushing by. Now it may seem odd to some that I would have my morning prayer in a coffee shop, but as an extrovert, I am often the most present to myself and to the Holy when I am surrounded by the energy of others. It is just a fact. I have tried to make it otherwise, spending my time distracted in quiet places, forcing myself to pay attention to the silence. While I do need these moments of solitude to remain grounded, I receive a very needed connection in the presence of others, much like a cord plugged into an electrical outlet.

Reading this prayer slowly to myself as I watched the beginning of a new day, I was aware of how each person I saw, including myself, was in the same boat. We were all starting the same day. The sun had recently come up in the eastern sky; the autumn leaves were blowing in the terrific wind outside in the street. Possibility was all around.

And yet as I looked out at the young man waiting for the bus at the stop across the street, I wondered what the possibility of his day really held. He looked tired, disheveled. And the two women sitting at the table nearby who were in intense conversation about what appeared to be something deeply important to them. What bound them together in such rich conversation? And the young coffee barista, the one that always remembers my "regular," flirting coyly with her beloved across the counter. What did their day hold?

As the prayer indicates, each of us carries a certain darkness and suffering that is visible and invisible to others. The world also carries such a heaviness. But, if we allow ourselves, we can choose to glimpse "the light that exists in every person." I believe that as we glimpse that light, if we take a moment to fan that flame through our interactions or our prayers for that person, the light grows and illuminates not only the individual, but also the world. Too often we only allow ourselves to give energy to that darkness, that suffering. By averting our eyes, by ignoring the other, by simply not being present, we can miss the opportunity to bring out the light in another person's life. When we do, we miss the moment for "grace to find a home." In missing the opportunity of recognizing the depth of suffering and the immensity of joy in those with whom we travel life's path, we lose out on the chance to have grace rain down on us.

As a new day dawns, may we all find our eyes wide open with the chance . . . with the choice . . . of connecting to that enduring light that glows at the center of all Creation. Amidst life's dark streaks, to do anything else would really be a shame.

Practice

Light a candle and be present to the light it brings to your space. Offer a prayer today for all those experiencing moments of darkness. Hold the light of the candle out toward those for whom you pray. Bring the candle to your own self and be mindful of the light within.

Have You?

They say that one of the reasons for tragedy is that you learn important lessons from it . . . appreciation for your normal life for one thing . . . a new longing for things only ordinary . . . the feeling is that we are so caught up in minutiae, slicing tomatoes, and filling out forms and waiting in lines and emptying the dryer and looking in the paper for things to do. That we forget how to use what we've been given. Therefore we don't taste the plum. We are blind to the slant of the four o'clock sun against the changing show of leaves. We are deaf to the throaty purity of children's voices. We are assumed to be rather hopeless. Swallowed up by incorrect notions divorced from the original genius with which we are born. Lost within days of living this distracting life. We are capable only of moments of single seconds of true appreciation and connection. That is the thought. – ELIZABETH BERG, *Range of Motion*

Recently, our girl's book club at church asked our women's book club to tell them our favorite beginning paragraph of a book. These words by Elizabeth Berg from one of her many novels continues to be one of my favorites. Of all the "great books" this might not appear on people's lists, but for my money this opening paragraph nearly says it all. I have used these words in sermons, as a meditation, and continue to return to its inherent truth.

This past week I read it once again and allowed the words to seep into the crevasses that had been made by the death of a dear person in my life. For the past four months I, and so many others, have followed the tragedy of her journey with ovarian cancer. Each day her husband religiously (and I do not use this word lightly) wrote of her struggles, her triumphs, her joys, and the tragedy that was gripping their family. He also wrote of the deep wisdom that grew out of this rich soil. Each day I logged onto her Caringbridge site to electronically share in the journey. I was privileged to witness her pictures and her family's pictures as they traveled this difficult road with grace, faith, sorrow, and immense joy.

Each day, after sending up a prayer for them all, I would remind myself of the gifts of my own life. I tried to remember to be present to the beauty around me, to really look at the food I was eating, to notice its colors and savor the tastes on my tongue. I looked into the eyes of the enormous black dog that lives in our house and saw the unconditional love there. I welcomed the pleasure of walking with my husband, having dinner with my sons, and talking with neighbors about mundane things. I tried not to live the distracted life. Always a challenge, don't you think?

This is, as Berg points out, the gift of tragedy. Of course, I did not experience this in the deep, powerful way those much closer to my friend had. But its wisdom was not lost on me, and, I hope, my attention to living was somehow a testament to my friend's grace-filled passing from this earth.

The first day I met her, I pulled my mini-van up behind hers for what would be countless soccer games to follow. Her bumper sticker read: *"Have You Thanked God Today?"* It is odd that nearly ten years have passed and I still remember that. Today the answer is yes. I thank God for her life. I thank God for the reminder. I thank God.

Practice

Begin a gratitude list today. At breakfast, write down five things for which you are grateful as you begin the day. At lunchtime, jot down five more things that have happened since breakfast that fill you with gratitude. At dinner, write down five more things for which you are thankful. As you get ready for sleep, look over what you have written. Let your heart be full.

Sacred Journey

With a deepening focus, keen preparation, attention to the path below our feet, and respect for the destination at hand, it is possible to transform even the most ordinary trip into a sacred journey, a pilgrimage. – PHIL COUSINEAU, *The Art of Pilgrimage*

This morning began in joy. I met for breakfast with the other leaders of a pilgrimage I will be privileged to take in October to Scotland. This adventure has been more than a year in the making and, as most adventures do, began with a passing statement of "Wouldn't it be great . . . ?" We had all had a desire to travel to the island of Iona and several other recognized holy sites in this loveliest of British lands. The passing statement began to take on flesh, and here we are only a few weeks away from what we pray will be a transforming experience for all involved. As the details get more refined and the seeds of hope become more deeply planted, I am recognizing the richness of what this journey might offer. The trick is to prepare just well enough to relieve anxiety while remaining open and receptive to the surprises, the movement of the Spirit that will travel alongside each pilgrim. It will be a balancing act for sure, but one that if held gently enough, will deliver us all back to our ordinary lives changed forever.

To think of oneself as a pilgrim seems an ancient term, an ancient endeavor. And yet, if we honor the way in which we travel each day in the companionship of the Holy, every day is a pilgrimage and we are all pilgrims on the daily Earth path. How might your day be different if you saw it that way? How might your work day unfold if, instead of the same old daily grind, you stepped out your door with the hope of a pilgrim heart? It is something to think about, isn't it ? Think of how meetings might be approached if we all sat down with the idea of being not just a worker but a pilgrim in search of transformation? Or how might we experience the

load of laundry thrown into the washer in the early morning hours before work if we thought of the act as preparing our clothes for the important journey ahead? How might we eat our breakfast or our lunch with attention to the steps along the sacred path? And how much better falling into bed at night might feel if we had the opportunity to reflect on what we experienced as holy in the ordinary living out of the day?

These are all pilgrim questions available to us with the rising of the sun each morning. It is up to each one of us whether or not we pick up the gauntlet and deeply focus our attention, being present to the path of our feet and finally giving proper respect to the destination at hand.

Pilgrim or not? You choose. But with the choice comes the prospect of being changed forever. Are you up for it?

Practice

Prepare for the day as if you are a pilgrim. Pack your bag with intention, openness, hope, grace, courage. See the world as a new adventure. Practice doing this over and over.

Shaking Eyeballs

Now there are a variety of gifts, but the same Spirit; and there are varieties of services, but the same God; and there are varieties of activities, but it is the same God who activates all of them in everyone. – 1 CORINTHIANS 12:4-6

Yesterday I spent the first part of the morning being a helper with Vacation Bible School. My role was to be a shepherd of sorts for the group known as the "Dandelions." I met them as they sat on a pale green quilt laid out on the floor where they were having their morning gathering time. The Dandelions ranged in age from five to seven years, and they had yellow name tags hanging around their necks. While waiting for the official gathering time to begin, we leisurely discussed whether the dandelion was a flower or a weed. Everyone had an opinion and expressed it with great passion. It was clear that no consensus would be made on this horticultural issue and so the conversation soon petered out.

Just then one of the girls turned to me and made this statement: "I can shake my eyeballs." Her declaration was pure, simple, and to the point. I tried to keep my expression neutral. "Really?" I said. "Yes," she returned and then began to somehow make her eyeballs shake back and forth from side to side without moving her head an inch. Seeing that I was clearly impressed, she smiled.

What to say to such a feat? I commented with the first thing that came to my mind: "How did you first realize you could do this?" She paused for a very long time and then said, "I don't know," as if the mystery of it all was answer enough. This gift which she had discovered at some point of her young life just was. She was a "girl who could shake her eyeballs." It was simply a part of who she was. There was no memory of how she came to try this. No memory of practicing in front of a mirror till she got it right. It was just a gift she possessed.

I carried that image with me all day. Those sweet, little blue eyes wiggling back and forth framed by her pale, blond hair that had not been completely combed before her morning arrival. I thought of all the gifts people have and how I am so often blessed to observe them or, even better, to be a recipient of those seeds planted deep within them. I think of the people I know who have such a gift for hospitality, how they make me feel as if they are so glad I am in their presence, how they mirror God's movement in the world. I think of those who have the gift of teaching, of leading young and old into a discovery of information and transformation. I think of those I know who have the gift of administration, keeping systems moving, details covered. I think of those who have the gift of music, of art, of storytelling, of opening the world to others in profound ways. So many gifts. So many ways to share them.

Like the girl who could shake her eyeballs, most often we are unaware of how we came to act on our gifts. It was simply something we tried once, were led to do by a force that is unseen but felt. The Spirit perhaps? I think so. But the result is always the same when gifts are shared. The giver and receiver are blessed, and the world seems a little brighter, is healed in some way.

What are your gifts? Have you shared them lately? Today is a good day to offer what you have and to brighten the world. It might even include a little shaking!

Practice

Take an inventory of your gifts. What brings you life? Joy? Happiness? What needs do you see around you? Where do your gifts meet the world's needs?

Well-Being

The Celtic theologian, poet, and wisdom-carrier John Philip Newell often speaks about "the healing of the world." I have been thinking about this phrase a lot this week. On Tuesday at our staff meeting, another wise man I know spoke of the United Methodist notion of "going on to perfection" and the difficulty he has had in giving flesh to these words, this concept. John Wesley, the founder of Methodism, often said that as Christians we are "going on to perfection." Since I, too, have had difficulty with this concept, these words, I listened intently to the content of the conversation searching for further understanding.

Sometime over the years I have begun to translate this concept of perfection into "going on toward wholeness." For me, this is more helpful, less full of baggage. Perfection has such a heavy cross to bear in our twenty-first century culture. Ads of "perfect" bodies, "perfect" homes, "perfect" relationships spring to mind. This is, I am fairly sure, not what John Wesley had in mind. But wholeness, shaping my life, my walk in faith, in a way that leads me home to the original wholeness from which I was born, that makes sense to me. And, most days, it seems even doable.

I am pretty sure that wholeness and healing go hand in hand. In a world that is splintered by so many factions, so much "us" and 'them," "right" and left," "included" and "excluded," wholeness would certainly be a goal to pursue. If we believe that we are created in the image of God, which I do, that pursuit toward wholeness and, eventually, holiness seems a noble endeavor.

And how to do that? I don't really have the complete answer. But I am sure that some attention to compassion, justice, humility, and kindness is in order. These are not qualities that are celebrated in the advertising world of perfection. But they are qualities that were lifted up by Jesus and other prophets of God as the way in which we bring healing to the world and wholeness to ourselves. Embracing

these goals may not help any of us fit into a size six pair of jeans or keep the wrinkles from aging our faces. But setting our intention to live a life of kindness and compassion, following a path of justice and humility, just might bring about a better world. And somehow I think that would be worth it.

In one of his prayers Newell writes: *"Grant me the grace to reclaim these depths, to uncover this treasure, to liberate these longings, and in being set free in my own spirit, to act for the well-being of the world."* Sign me up.

Practice

What wholeness do you long for? Take the prayer of Newell and pray it at the beginning of your day and at day's end. Perhaps this becomes your prayer for the week, the month, the year.

What We Weave

The words we weave can become a web in which we also are bound. Once uttered, these words cannot be called back; they fly out on the winds until they find their target. In a tradition that recognizes the power of words, we also maintain a watch upon our tongue, lest it speak words that we will regret.
– CAITLIN MATTHEWS, *The Celtic Spirit*

When I read these words in my morning devotion today, my mother's voice rang out loud and clear in my head: "If you can't say something nice, don't say anything at all!" How many times over the years had she heard me heading over a cliff from which I might not be able to return, only to caution me about the power of words?

Just this past week I was flipping from channel to channel on the television, looking for something to entertain me for an hour. I was struck with the raw and angry language that was being bantered between people. I finally turned it off. The same thing can happen on the radio. I once listened faithfully to a station that mostly just made me laugh. It did not have any redeeming educational value whatsoever, but each show was filled with silliness. But over the last year, that same station has turned some dark corner, and it seems all the hosts need to lash out, take cheap jabs at people, exhibit a general mean-spiritedness. I have chosen to take them off my listening lineup.

Unkind words can also be found in emails, that instant form of communication where we can rant and rave and hit send without any effort at self-censoring. It is quite common to get these forms of communications. Sometimes they are followed by an apology in which the sender recognizes that, if they had only taken the time to reflect on their words, they would have chosen their words more wisely and not have hit "send" so quickly.

I am of the belief that words are so powerful they find a home in our bodies, affecting our day, our sense of self, our lives. I believe this to be true because I have

had it happen to me. Words spoken unkindly, cavalierly, have nearly made me physically ill. Has this happened to you? It is difficult to bound back from, isn't it?

What we say to another person is important, whether we are speaking about issues of ultimate concern—life, death, love, forgiveness—or the mundane—please pass the salt, how much are these bananas? How we choose our words just might makes all the difference in the world to another person. This is something not to be taken lightly.

May we all be surrounded this day by beautiful, kind, and loving words. May all the words that come out of our mouths, or through our fingers, be ones we are proud to speak into the air or have printed on paper. May all the words we weave, spoken and received, be ones that bring the greater good to an already hurting world.

Practice

Thank before you speak today. Are the words about to be said ones that harm or help? With the words spoken be remembered as kind or harsh? Will what is said to another lift them up or tear them down? Choose wisely.

Uphill Both Ways

Does the road wind uphill all the way?
Yes, to the very end.
Will the journey take the whole long day?
From morn to night, my friend. – CHRISTINA ROSSETTI

Every parent has no doubt told the story to a whining child about "walking to school in the snow, uphill both ways." It is a joke of course but never fails to stop the complaining in its tracks, for at least a moment, as the logic of this concept tries to sink in. And yet many of us have had the experience of traveling uphill with no end in sight, feeling that, indeed, we are traveling uphill both ways.

As I continue to prepare for my October pilgrimage to the island of Iona in Scotland, I am thinking of travel, of walking, in both metaphorical and practical ways.

There is, of course, the issue of the right shoes to wear. As a self-professed shoe junkie, this has brought no shortage of anxiety. But now that I think I have that problem solved, I can concentrate on the deeper meanings of what it means to walk the path of this long-awaited adventure, this journey.

Last week our group of pilgrims gathered for a final briefing by the trip planners. We shared details, a wonderful meal, and a combined anticipation for what these eleven days together will bring. As I looked around the room, I tried to imagine the many reasons and life circumstances each person was bringing to this road that may, at times, feel like an uphill trek. Some of my fellow pilgrims I know very well, and we have a long history. Others I am still getting to know, learning their names, hoping that the days spent together on buses and planes and around shared food and rich experiences will bring new friends. I am hoping that by journey's end I will know more about each person, will come to a place of gratitude for having shared the road together, from morning till night, "the whole day long."

But one does not need to be preparing for a long trip to embrace the words of Christina Rossetti. Each day provides its own journey, uphill and down. Each stage of our lives also offers this gift: a road that is to be traveled without our knowing where the twists and turns will take us. All the plans we make can turn on a dime. Anyone who has lived more than a few years knows this. What seemed like a smooth moving, carefree existence can suddenly turn into an uphill battle with an unforeseen diagnosis, a deep loss, a turn too quickly made. This is the nature of life. Each day is a journey of its own if we lean into the ever-increasing rays of sunlight.

And so for all those who are held in the limbo of an uphill journey, may prayers hold you. For all those who cannot see the path ahead or are too frightened to look, may prayers surround you. For those who travel alone and long for companionship, may prayers embrace you. From morn to night. From night to morn.

Practice

Take time to notice the journey you are taking this day. Take time, also, to notice your fellow travelers. Look into their eyes. Choose to be a comfort, a guide, a friend, a companion. From morn till night.

Happiness

Happiness. I have been thinking a lot about happiness lately. I have even been asking people if they are happy. Try it some time. You get surprising results. I am not sure what prompted this examination of happiness. Perhaps it was the recognition that I don't, perhaps, laugh as much as I once did. It was an odd discovery about myself. I think of myself as happy most of the time. But when I realized that, in truth, I do not laugh as often as I once did, it was a kind of wake-up call. So, I have been doing a personal survey of happiness.

"Happiness grows only in the sweet soil of time," writes Wayne Muller in his book *Sabbath.*

> *As our time is eaten away by speed and overwork, we are less available to be surprised by joy, a sunset, a kind word, an unplanned game of tag with a child, a warm loaf of bread from the oven. But for all our striving and accomplishments, our underlying need for happiness does not withdraw and disappear. So we pursue happiness on the run, trying to make our lives more and more efficient, squeezing every task into tighter increments, hoping to somehow "get" our happiness when we are able to fit it in.*

That pretty much sums up my daily life. How about yours?

Yesterday I was zooming through a neighborhood in St. Paul when a lawn sign caught my eye. "What if there is more to life?" the sign read. I nearly threw on my brakes, hoping to read the smaller print that lay below the large, bold letters of this compelling question. What could this possibly be an advertisement for? Who would put this sign on their lawn? I looked for others like it as I sped along, hoping it was some kind of neighborhood conspiracy to wake us all up to ourselves. What if there is MORE to life? And just what is "more"?

Well, I suppose everyone would answer the "more" question differently. For some, more is knowing they have enough food to feed their children and the money to pay their rent. But I think the source of this question is more existential than that. I have a feeling it ties back into my own happiness question. What does it mean to live a life well, one that brings happiness? What does it mean for you?

It is said that the Buddha equated the spiritual life with a life of happiness. He was often known to offer blessings of loving kindness with the words, "May you be happy." Oddly enough, on the Fourth of July I happened upon a copy of the Declaration of Independence and read the words written by those who dreamed our country into being, lifting high the goal of "the pursuit of happiness." Our very existence as citizens of this country was shaped by the notion of happiness.

These warm summer days can provide time for ruminating over many things. What better thing to allow our minds to roll around than the state of happiness? Are you happy? Are you making room for happiness to walk in and ask you to dance, to make you laugh? If you, too, have been considering your own happiness, I invite you to join me in the pursuit of this spiritual life. And may our searching contain a few good belly laughs.

Practice

Ask yourself the question: "Am I happy?" Allow your answer to guide your next steps. Make a point of asking those around you the same question. Listen carefully to their answers. Include them in your prayers.

Staying Alive

Seize life! Eat bread with gusto,
Drink wine with a robust heart.
Oh yes—God takes pleasure in your pleasure!
Dress festively every morning.
Don't skimp on colors or scarves.
Relish life with the spouse you love
Each and every day of your precarious life.
Each day is God's gift. It's all you get in exchange
For the hard work of staying alive.
Make the most of each one!
Whatever turns up, grab it and do it. And heartily!
This is your last and only chance at it,
For there's neither work to do nor thought to think
In the company of the dead, where you're most certainly headed.
– ECCLESIASTES 9:7-10

This was the scripture one of my colleagues read for devotions at our staff meeting yesterday. In the course of all I did during the hours that followed that meeting, I kept thinking back to these words, this interpretation of scripture in Eugene Peterson's *The Message*. What a *carpe diem*, seize the day, message! It made me question the little things that wanted to nag at my spirit, to let them go in favor of embracing the last and only chance at this gift of a day.

While most people are somewhat familiar with the words of Ecclesiastes 3, "for everything there is a season," most don't read through much of the rest of the book. They know this text, not so much from Sunday school, but from the lyrics of the Byrd's song, "Turn, Turn, Turn," and subsequent remakes of that recording through different generations. Ecclesiastes is a part of the Wisdom literature in

the Bible, words meant to provide wisdom and guidance for life in the real world. And Ecclesiastes 9 does this as well as any self-help book you might pull off the shelf at Barnes & Noble: "Seize life! Eat and drink heartily. Put on your best and brightest clothes. Today is God's gift, never to be relived. Take what the day brings and find a place of gratitude in it." In my opinion, it doesn't get much better, or wiser, than that.

Of course, like any good piece of wisdom, it does point out the obvious. This day is ours to create and live. What we make of it is the currency we use in exchange for the hard work that goes into it. I recognize that I read these words from a place of privilege and that there are those who do not have much say in what their day will hold, may not have the chance to eat or drink with gusto if at all, may have no choice in what clothes they wear. This understanding makes this scripture even more urgent to me. And of course, there is that bit about being in the "company of the dead." Sobering, huh?

So, today is already on its way, this gift from God is already unfolding before us. I've yet to decide what I'll wear today, but I promise it will be colorful and may even be completed with a scarf. And as I eat my lunch, I plan to savor each bite as if it were my last. I plan to pay attention to the relationships in my life that bring me joy and offer love in return. At day's end I hope to be able to hand over the hard work of this day as payment for staying alive.

It simply seems like the wise way to live.

Practice

Each day can begin with intention. What are your intentions for this gift of a day? How will you savor it? How will you celebrate living? Set your intention and give thanks.

Kindness

My religion is very simple. My religion is kindness. – THE DALAI LAMA

For some reason I have been thinking about kindness lately. To put it plainly, I realized that I have been in several settings in which kindness was in short supply, where people chose hurtful rather than helpful words. I recognize that it had begun to nag at my soul. So when I was at a restaurant yesterday and I was about to move a chair to sit down and a young man turned and smiled at me and, instead, moved the chair for me, I somehow was stunned by his effort. It seems simple enough, I know, but with all the jagged edges that were sticking out of my skin, it seemed the sweetest, gentlest of actions. I was melted by his kindness.

Sometime last week, I listened to a report on Minnesota Public Radio about the civility or lack thereof in our culture right now. There were many reasons given for this phenomenon, not the least of which was our ability to communicate with others via email and other social networks which don't require face-to-face connections. It feels quite safe to say whatever comes to our minds and hit send without any personal responsibility to the impact of our words. We react quickly, sometimes rashly, and pass on our words in the blink of an eye. All without the benefit of seeing the flinch of another, the grimace that crosses a face, or even the tear that might roll down a cheek. With all the positive ease this form of communication brings to our lives, this is one of the true downfalls.

Kindness. Who comes to your mind when you think of "kindness"? A parent? A teacher? A neighbor? Your child? A dear friend? Have you known the kindness of strangers in your life? Have you been extended the hospitality of kindness? I hope so. I hope there are many people who come to mind who have been bearers of kindness. Sometimes it is a surprising gift, like the young man who moved the chair, his face all full of smiles. And then there are those times when you know you

will be walking into kindness. You look forward to it, like a special holiday meal, and anticipate its healing properties. I can think of a couple of retreat centers I have frequented where kindness seems to seep out of the very walls.

This morning I learned that one of the kindest men I know had passed yesterday from this life to the next. It was a blow. He was someone who walked into a room and kindness seemed to float off his words, his movements, his very being, like proverbial fairy dust. Though he was older and had tenuous health, it was still difficult to hear of his passing, to imagine the world without his signature grace and goodness.

Kindness. It can seem an elusive thing most days. But, perhaps, the real lesson is that we each carry this magic fairy dust. The discipline is to use it. Often. And always.

Practice

Choose kindness this day. Offer kindness first to yourself. What might that look like to you? Offer kindness to your family and co-workers. Especially, offer kindness to the strangers you meet. Some have met an angel in doing so.

Walking Meditation

The last several days have been jam-packed with wonderful things—sons arriving home from college; beautiful, inspiring music at worship; plans for summer events; graduation parties; and the anticipation of summer activities and all the plans that need to be made for them. When you pile all this onto the regular demands of daily life it can be, truth be told, a whirlwind. I, of course, recognize that this is pure blessing. There are many people who would love to have this manner of activity flowing into their lives. And so I don't mean for my words to be complaint, simply report.

Late Thursday afternoon I was on my way to a graduation party between a day of work and an evening meeting. I had decided to take the scenic route along Lake of the Isles and Lake Calhoun in hopes of having a few moments of quiet, slower driving. Going along the lakes, the frenzy of the day began to slide away as I watched joggers, bicyclists, and frisbee players enjoying the cloudy, though dry day. Young children climbed all over the playground that sits on the shore of the lake as they began to live into the freedom of summer. Walkers made their way around the lakes, talking animatedly with their companions.

As my eyes strayed away from the lake, I looked toward the back garden of the Zen Center that faces the lake. What I saw caused me to nearly slam on my brakes as I glimpsed six to eight people doing walking meditation. Their bodies were moving so slowly that they seemed like statues except for the ever-so-slight movement of an arm, a hand, a head, a foot. Their eyes were intently focused as the tiniest muscles propelled them at a slower than tortoise-like gait. The sheer beauty and silence of their pace stunned me out of the nature of the movement of my fast-moving day. I wanted to pull over, abandon my car like one who had been "raptured," and join in their slow, deliberate, breath-filled movements. My whole body was filled with such deep longing for what they had!

Over the last several days, I have thought so many times of what I witnessed on Thursday and the deep longing it placed within me. I don't know if I'd ever be able to slow down to that kind of pace or not, but I'd sure like to try. For some reason, when I have thought of those practicing this walking meditation, I have kept thinking of the insect, the praying mantis. Have you ever observed the slow, deliberate movements of these green, stick-like creatures? I remembered the summer my brother captured several and kept them in jars for our curious child selves to ponder. I would stare into their eyes, the multi-faceted lenses that seemed far too big for their faces. Why had the walking meditation triggered that in my memory?

Then today, as I was searching for a poem of healing for an upcoming worship service, I saw these words: *"May my body be a prayerstick for the world."* I have no idea who Joan Halifax is, or why she wrote these words, but somehow I think she must have seen humans practicing walking meditation. We must be kindred spirits.

For all those who walk their prayers slowly, like sticks, and for those who rush by, like fireflies, may we all offer our prayers to the world, as we learn from one another the power of the walking. So be it.

Practice

Walking meditation is not difficult nor something you need training to do. Simply pay attention to the steps of your own path. You may want to walk at a slower pace than your normal rhythm. Notice how your foot touches the ground. Notice your breath while you move. Be fully present to the gift of movement.

Vigil

Vigil: a purposeful or watchful staying awake during the usual hours of sleep; a watch kept; the evening or day before a festival, or the devotional services held then.
– WEBSTER'S NEW WORLD COLLEGE DICTIONARY

The word "vigil" has been floating through my brain for the last twenty-four hours. I had the privilege yesterday of sitting vigil with a family whose loved one is teetering between this earthly life and the next. The silence, the prayers, the scriptures spoken, the stories told, the tears and the laughter—all created a nest in which the dying one was held. Each of us represented a twig, a piece of grass, a feather creating this nest that was bound together with unspoken love. We sat suspended in time, keeping watch, full of devotion. It was a holy time in which the presence of the Sacred breathed with us.

Vigil. It is not a word we use often. And yet we have all, at one time or another, held vigil or have been held in vigil. Anyone who is a parent has probably spent more than one night at the bedside of a sick child. As we kept watch, we have mopped their feverish brow with a cold cloth, told stories to keep them calm and comforted, held cups of cool water to quench their thirst. As adults we can probably remember when we were younger, coming home after having been out too late, to find a parent sitting quietly on the couch, the television blinking in the darkness. Someone had sat a vigil of protection over our lives that night, having devoted their lives to watching over ours.

Many gardeners are, right now, sitting a kind of vigil over the plants they put into the ground earlier this spring. With watchful eyes and hopeful palates, they wait for tomatoes, green beans, corn, raspberries. While the work of weeding and watering gives the human something to do, the vigil kept is about being in some

kind of relationship with the living green things that will nurture human bodies. The vigil is really about nurturing the soul.

I imagine those who have relatives serving our country keep vigil. Watching the news, listening for reports of the areas in which they know their loved ones to be. Perhaps they keep a photo of their father, mother, child, sister, or brother, spouse or partner in a special place. Perhaps they even create an altar with a vigil light that is lit in an effort of protection and filled with prayers. It is a vigil that is filled with love, fear, and great hope.

Still others I know have sat vigil over a pet that is old, ill, and dying. I remember one September night five years ago as our son and I kept vigil over the family dog who had begun to have seizures. We knew in our hearts that he was dying, but we didn't want to believe it. And so we lay on the floor on each side of him, reaching out our hands when another uncontrollable contraction of muscles gripped his furry, loved body. It was one of the sweetest, saddest nights of devotion, of keeping watch, I can remember.

For what have you kept vigil? Who has kept vigil over you? Though it is a word that seems old, from another time, its action is necessary for the ongoing relationships we all hold. And may it always be so.

Practice

Choose something or someone to hold in vigil. Allow your energy and prayers to form a cloak of love and protection around the image or presence of this being. Ask God's blessing upon them and you.

Thank You

A special thank you to the amazing Barbara Brandt, artist and designer for the book cover art for *The Practicing Life*. I am so grateful for her listening and creative spirit and the laughter we shared. I am also so grateful to Karen Walhof of Kirk House Publishers for her support, generosity and encouragement. A full heart goes out to the readers of Pause, the blog that gave birth to many of these reflections. Your responses and encouragement were always a gift. Thank you, as always, to the people of Hennepin Avenue United Methodist Church in Minneapolis, Minnesota. Your faith, your generous spirit, and your companionship on the journey continue to hold my life.

As always, the three men in my life, Dan, Colin and Evan, have inspired my practicing life and showered me with such love. For this I am filled to overflowing. Finally, to my Mom, Eva, who gave me the love of words and continues to walk this blessed path with me.